USS California

by David Doyle

A Visual History of the Golden State Battleship BB-44

Table of Contents

Published by
Ampersand Group, Inc.
A HobbyLink Japan company
235 NE 6th Ave., Suite B
Delray Beach, FL 33483-5543
561-266-9686 • 561-266-9786 Fax
www.ampersandpubco.com • www.hlj.com

HobbyLink Japan

Acknowledgements

This book could not have been created without the considerable assistance of many friends, colleagues and institutions. This includes Tom Kailbourn, Tracy White, Dana Bell, Dave Baker, Jerry Leslie, Roger Torgeson, Sean Hert, Rick Davis, Scott Taylor, James Noblin, the staff of the Naval History and Heritage Command, Puget Sound Naval Shipyard, the National Archives and Records Administration branches in Washington DC, College Park, MD, San Bruno, California and Seattle, Washington, the Mare Island Museum, Vallejo Naval and Historical Museum, San Diego Air and Space Museum, and the San Francisco Maritime National Historical Park. Most of all, I thank my wonderful wife Denise, who located and copied thousands of pages of original, primary source documents and scanned hundreds of photos.

Photo credits: National Archives (NARA), Library of Congress (LOC), National Park Service, San Diego Air and Space Museum, Mare Island Museum, Vallejo Naval and Historical Museum, Naval History and Heritage Command and US Navy.

Color profiles by Claudio Fernandez. Photos colorized by Claudio Fernandez and Atsushi Yamashita. Line art by Todd Sturgell.

Front cover: The USS *California* underway on 23 August 1935. Also see page 67. Original photo colorized by Claudio Fernandez.

Title page: Her clipper bow pushing back a sizable wave, *California* makes a speed run off San Francisco in late 1921. The *California* would be an active unit of the U.S. Navy in the Pacific through 1945, albeit spending 108 days resting on the floor of Pearl Harbor following the Japanese attack of 7 December, 1941. (Mare Island Museum)

Back cover: USS *California* at anchor in Sinclair Inlet off the Navy Yard Puget Sound on 28 April 1945. Also see page 145. Original photo colorized by Atsushi Yamashita.

Right: *California's* official mascot was a five-week-old cinnamon bear cub found in Yosemite National Park. The bear was named "Yosemite Prunes." The ship eventually gained the nickname "Prune Barge," reportedly because the State of California was a major producer of the fruit. (Mare Island Museum)

Introduction

The battleship *California* that is the subject of this book was the fifth warship to bear the name of the Golden State. Its predecessors included a Civil War-designed screw sloop, and two converted yachts that bore the name during the 19-teens. But the battleship's most significant predecessor was the armored cruiser *California*, ACR/CA-6). Authorized by the Naval Building Act of 1899, the cruiser was the last of three armored cruisers included in that act, and was the one specified, "...be built on or near the coast of the Pacific Ocean." Union Iron Works in San Francisco launched the ship on 28 April 1904, but due to the San Francisco earthquake of 1906, commissioning ceremonies were not held until 1 August 1907, delayed her fitting out.

The 13,680-ton warship spent much of her life plying the Pacific waters off the California coast, although in 1911-1912 she did steam for Honolulu, and then on to China, Japan and the Philippines. On 1 September 1914, in preparation for the keel laying of a new *California*

the next month, the cruiser was renamed, becoming the *San Diego*.

After the United States entered WWI, *San Diego* transited the Panama Canal in July 1918, joining the Atlantic Fleet, becoming flagship of the Commander, Cruiser Force, Atlantic Fleet. While *San Diego* did venture to France once, in November 1917, most of her time was devoted to serving as coastal escort for convoys. On 19 July 1918 while on routine voyage from Portsmouth, New Hampshire to New York, *San Diego* struck a German-laid mine in the waters off Sandy Hook. The cruiser sank in only 28 minutes, taking with her six of her crew. Fortunately 1,183 survivors were rescued.

In the early years of the 20th century the battleship represented not only the pinnacle of a nation's military might, but also was the crowning part of the nation's technical prowess. New concepts were carefully studied, and if deemed meritorious, incorporated into new construction. With some much prestige, as well as money, at stake, change was often slow. When the designs for "Battleship 1915" were being proposed during May 1913, some of these concepts concerned propulsion, with reciprocating steam engines being the norm. However, geared turbines had been tried, and turboelectric drive had been successfully tested in the collier

Jupiter. Based on that success, on 17 October 1914 the Bureau of Engineering suggested one of the three "Battleship 1915" vessels be completed with turboelectric drive, and become the navy's first all-electric battleship.

On 14 October the keel of that first all-electric battleship was laid with considerable ceremony. Naval Constructor George H. Rock drove a nickel-plated rivet that joined two heavy pieces of steel, while Brooklyn Navy Yard Commandant Nathanial Usher announced to Secretary of the Navy Josephus Daniels: "Mr. Secretary, the keel of the *California* has been well and truly laid!"

However, the vessel rising from the ways in New York, in the shadow of Battleship 39, the ill-fated *Arizona*, would be renamed.

There had been a movement for some time to build a battleship on the west coast, with Mare Island Navy Yard lobbying assistant Secretary of the Navy Franklin Roosevelt for this honor. The Yard had demonstrated a consistent ability to meet financial and scheduling deadlines, and also to work more economically than some east coast yards.

Congress authorized constructions of two "Battleship 1916" vessels on 3 March 1915, which stated: "The President is hereby

USS *California* (BB-44) was the fifth USN ship or vessel to bear that name. This is the second such ship, the armored cruiser USS *California* (ACR-6), launched in April 1904. Later she was renamed *San Diego* to allow the battleship to be named *California*. (NARA)

authorized to have constructed two first-class battleships carrying as heavy armor and as powerful armament as any vessel of their class, to have the highest practicable speed and greatest desirable radius of action, and to cost, exclusive of armor and armament, not to exceed $7,800,000 each..." Bids were solicited, with bid opening on 17 November 1915. Bids were received from three navy yards as well as three private contractors. As it turned out, navy yards provided better bids for construction of battleships 43 and 44 than did private yards.On 8 December 1915, Secretary Daniels announced that the Navy had awarded a contract to build battleship hull number 44 to the Mare Island yard. Hull number 44 was one of two "Battleship 1916" vessels to be built. Almost immediately the public and politicians seized on the idea that it would be fitting that the Mare Island-built battleship should be California. Editorials, letters, and even a joint resolution by the California state legislature urged Secretary Daniels to make this so. Finally, on 14 March 1916 Daniels announced that the California, hull number 40, under construction in Brooklyn, would be renamed New Mexico, and battleship 44 would be California. California's sister ship, battleship 43, the Tennessee, would be built in Brooklyn.

In order to make Mare Island ready for construction of the massive hull, buildings had to be moved and shipways extended by 100 feet. In fact, yard improvements would consume $460,000

of the $7,248,456 that Mare Island had bid for the job. On 25 October 1916 a keel was again laid for a battleship named California.

The contracts were modified after award, but before construction began. A turboelectric drive system planned for Battleship 1917 was advanced into the Battleship 1916 projects. Redesign of the hulls began accordingly on 13 December 1915. In February it was decided to include a four-layer torpedo protection system, requiring further redesign.

The armament of the ships would essentially duplicate those of the previous Battleship 1915; that is twelve 14-inch rifles, and a secondary battery of 5-inch guns, all mounted above the forecastle deck, as well as deck-mounted antiaircraft guns.

Armor fourteen inches thick at its maximum and tapering to eight inches near the extreme turrets would protect the most critical portions of the machinery. The four main battery turrets, their faces protected by slabs of armor 18-inches thick, were to rest on barbettes made of 13-inch armor.

Tennessee was the lead vessel of the class of ships built to the "Battleship 1916" design, and Brooklyn was the lead yard. Hence, designs and blueprints were sent from the east coast to the west, which sometimes caused delays in construction. An even bigger delay came when the United States was drawn into WWI on 6 April 1917. Yard workers and facilities heretofore devoted to con-

struction of California were diverted to building and maintaining lesser vessels, most notably destroyers, involved in the prosecution of the war. It would be 20 November 1919 before California's hull was ready for launch–almost 37 months.

The construction of a warship, particularly during this era, was labor intensive at every level. The hand-drawn blueprints arrived at Mare Island, where they were sent to an area known as the mold loft. There, full-sized wooden patterns of the vessel's frames, ribs and other components were made. These patterns were then taken to the steel shops, where steel was formed to match the size and shape of the patterns. Those steel pieces, sometimes weighing hundreds of pounds, then were shuffled to the shipways, where a bevy of workers placed red-hot rivets, hammering the heads of each over in a back-backing, repetitious process.

Even as her hull began to rise over surrounding buildings at Mare Island, design changes came through. In 1919 the Chief of Naval Operations directed that Tennessee and California be equipped with facilities to serve as fleet flagships. Because construction of Tennessee was more advanced, and would be challenging to amend, this order was changed, directing that only California be so equipped. The changes were made, at a cost of $204,555 plus an additional $21,000 in engineering work.

An artist's rendering of the projected battleship California shows only one smokestack. The California and sister ship Tennessee would comprise the Tennessee Class, although when this drawing was made is was anticipated the class would be named California. (Library of Congress)

Above left: The official start of construction on the battleship USS *California* was the keel-laying ceremony at the Mare Island Navy Yard, Vallejo, California, on 25 October 1916. Presiding over the ceremony was Capt. F. M. Bennett, U.S. Navy, seen here. Civilian officials who participated included U.S. Senator James Phelan, who read a message from President Woodrow Wilson. **Top right:** Poised with riveting hammers and tongs at *California*'s keel-laying ceremony are, left to right, Captain Beach, Captain Gleason, Captain Reed, Captain Cheatham, Commander Cox, and master shipfitter Maroney. To their rear is the ship's keel at its inception. **Above right:** Mayors George Drusel of Napa and James Roney of Vallejo take turns swinging at rivets during the keel-laying ceremony. The ceremonial rivet work was predictably sloppy, and yard workers later removed those rivets and drove new rivets into the keel. (NARA, all)

2942 - U. S. S. CALIFORNIA

MARE ISLAND, CAL NOV. 16 1916

LOOKING FOR'D

3067 - U. S. S. CALIFORNIA

MARE ISLAND CAL   JAN. 16 1917

LOOKING AFT FROM BOW

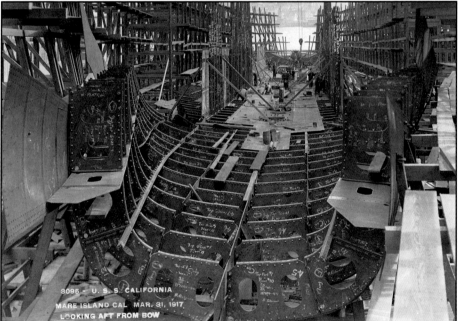

3095 - U. S. S. CALIFORNIA

MARE ISLAND CAL MAR. 31, 1917

LOOKING AFT FROM BOW

Left: Mare Island employees work alongside California's keel, which rests on the cribbing that will support the ever-increasing weight of the hull up to her launching. **Top Right:** The progress of construction is documented in a 16 January 1917 view from the bow. Steel plates of the shell, the outer skin of the hull, are in place in the foreground. Farther back, the frames are being constructed in sections, joined to the keel and to the shell. **Above right:** With Vallejo, California, visible across the Napa River in the background, more of the bow framing and shell have been installed by 31 March 1917. Frame sections, numbered consecutively from bow to stern, are marked for position and orientation. (NARA, all)

Above left: On the same date the preceding photo was taken, work on the *California* is observed from the stern facing forward. In the distance is a large crane for placing construction materials. In the foreground is the keel and some of the shell plates of the bottom of the stern are tacked together with nuts and bolts until they can be riveted.
Above right: Two weeks after the preceding view was taken, on 16 April 1917, the progress of work on the *California* is documented from atop the scaffold on the port side of the hull. In the foreground is the stern. Bulkheads to protect the machinery spaces, including the eight oil-burning boilers, are well underway amidships. Around those bulkheads are the upper plates of the double bottom. (NARA, both)

3304 - U.S.S. CALIFORNIA
MARE ISLAND CAL. JULY 2, 1917

3383 - U.S.S. CALIFORNIA
MARE ISLAND CAL. AUG. 21-1917-PLACING STERN POST

Above left: Taken from approximately the same vantage point as the preceding photo, this view from astern shows the progress of additional bulkhead installations on 2 July 1917. In the foreground, bulkhead number 135, one of the final ones before the stern, is under construction. A crane, seen under construction in the preceding view, has been erected in the right background.

Above right: On 21 August 1917, yard workers at Mare Island are employing an A-frame to lift and position the sternpost of the *California*. The sternpost is the rearmost vertical frame member of a ship, located at the longitudinal centerline. With the United States' entry in World War I four month earlier, priorities in the shipyards changed, and work on the *California* was slowing down. (NARA, both)

Above left: A comparison of this 2 October 1917 photo of *California* from astern with the similar one dated 2 July 1917 shows the extent to which work on the ship had slowed down. From this angle, there are virtually no distinguishable differences in the state of construction. The priorities of U.S. shipyards had shifted from constructing capital ships to building cargo ships and escort craft.

Above right: With World War I drawing toward its end, work on the *California* was proceeding, albeit slowly, as documented in this 1 October 1918 photograph taken from astern. Some advancement had taken place in the construction of the bulkheads forward of bulkhead 135 in the foreground since October 1917, and some steel decking had been installed in the stern since a year ago. (NARA, both)

Above left: By 1 December 1918, many lateral beams had been installed on the *California*. A door recently had been cut through the center of bulkhead 135 in the foreground, and two small ports had been cut through the same bulkhead to the starboard of that door. Several longitudinal frame members with lightening holes have been installed on the deck in the immediate foreground.

Above right: In the month since the preceding photo was taken, much steel decking has been installed on the third deck in this 1 January 1919 photograph. The partially completed curve in the deck for the barbette of turret four is in view; the smaller round opening in the deck with the guard rail is the opening for the barbette of turret three, which at this level below decks was smaller in diameter than barbette four. (NARA, both)

Top left: The area around the two aft barbettes is viewed from the port side of the third deck on 1 January 1919. Several hatches with wooden guard rails and ladders are in the foreground. At the bottom center is a portable rivet-heating furnace and several rivet barrels. **Top right:** In another 1 January 1919 view from the port side, steel deck plates have been installed over much of the area above the boilers in the amidships area. There were eight oil-burning Bureau Express boilers, each in its own watertight compartment. **Above left:** The *California*'s four 14-inch turrets are under construction at Mare Island on 1 March 1919. The cylindrical lower parts of the turrets have taken shape, but the gun houses on top are thus far restricted to the horizontal bottom plates and some interior plates. **Above right:** An armor deck plate in the background is about to be installed on the prepared area in the foreground. Caulk has been very methodically and neatly applied on the under layer of decking, with particular care to surround rivet holes to limit water infiltration. (NARA, all)

Above left: The third deck has been nearly completed, as viewed from astern on 1 April 1919, and the next deck above it is being started at the bow in the distance. The openings for the barbettes for turrets three and four with temporary guard rails in place are visible. Building materials, rivet furnaces and barrels, hoses, and gas cylinders, and other equipment litter the deck.

Above right: In a 5 June 1919 view from the stern, construction is now proceeding rapidly. The sides of the hull are advancing above the level of the third deck, and the upper, main, and second decks are under construction at the bow in the background. The prominent opening for barbette number four is in view, and the smaller opening for barbette three is a bit forward of it. (NARA, both)

Above left: One month after the preceding photo was taken, on 1 July 1919, framing for the main deck is in place at the stern in the foreground. Amidships, some of the lateral framing beams have been installed, but the third deck is still visible below them. Adjacent to the closer crane is a gangplank by which workmen entered the hull and carried in some of the lighter construction materials.

Above right: On 20 August 1919, workmen at Mare Island are placing the rudder assembly on the *California*. The men laboring to secure lines to the hoist cables at the top of the rudder provide a sense of scale of this massive assembly. To perform this operation, U.S. Navy Floating Crane No. 33, with a lifting capacity of 150 tons, was brought alongside the stern; it is in the background. (NARA, both)

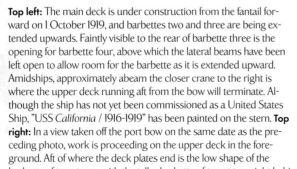

Top left: The main deck is under construction from the fantail forward on 1 October 1919, and barbettes two and three are being extended upwards. Faintly visible to the rear of barbette three is the opening for barbette four, above which the lateral beams have been left open to allow room for the barbette as it is extended upward. Amidships, approximately abeam the closer crane to the right is where the upper deck running aft from the bow will terminate. Although the ship has not yet been commissioned as a United States Ship, "USS *California* / 1916-1919" has been painted on the stern. **Top right:** In a view taken off the port bow on the same date as the preceding photo, work is proceeding on the upper deck in the foreground. Aft of where the deck plates end is the low shape of the barbette of turret one, with the taller barbette of turret two right behind it. **Above left:** With about six weeks to go until launching, propeller shafts are being installed on the starboard side of the *California* on 5 October 1919. The rudder is to the far left. Written all over the hull are reference data and inspector's marks: "Bianchi" appears frequently.

Above right: From left to right, viewed from the port side, are the barbettes for turrets three and four on 1 October 1919. Beams for the main deck have been left open over barbette four to leave space for its extension upward. The barbette armor was 14 to 16 inches thick. (NARA, all)

BUILDING OF THE
U.S.S. CALIFORNIA
MARE-ISLAND, CAL.

Top left: The four turrets for the *California* were still under construction on 1 October 1919 and were mounted on stands. They are viewed from their right rears, showing the cylindrical foundations, the base plates of the gun houses, and interior girder-type structures. **Top right:** The ammunition-handling rooms of the *California's* 14-inch gun turrets are resting on construction stands at Mare Island on 1 October 1919. After the ship was launched, these structures would be installed in the barbettes below the gun houses of the turrets. (NARA) **Above left:** The building ways where the *California* is under construction, center, are viewed from the Napa River not long before the ship was launched. The building with the twin towers, visible in several preceding photos, was the Mare Island ferry house and slip. (NARA) **Above right:** With only 18 days to go

until launching, the rush is on to get the *California* ready for the water. The hull has been painted, and staging planks are suspended at various parts of the hull. The gaping hole in the deck marks where the barbette of turret number one will eventually rise. Aft of it, barbette two stands well above the upper deck. At this point, this deck comprises steel plates; wooden planking will be installed on it during the post-launching fitting-out period. (Mare Island Museum)

Above left: The bow of the *California* presents a sleek, thoroughly modern aspect in a photograph taken a week before the launching, 12 November 1919. Draft marks for gauging how deep in the water the ship was riding were painted on each side of the bow. Of the five openings in the bow, the two small upper ones were bullnoses, for mooring lines, and the three large ones were hawsepipes, for accommodating the anchor chains as well as the anchors, when raised. **Top right:** The *California* is viewed from the front over navy yard buildings in early November 1919. The large light-colored area on the hull marks where the armored belt will be installed during the fitting-out process. A torpedo port is below the waterline. **Above right:** Four days before the launching, on 16 November 1919 the right side of the bow poppet is visible. The ship was fitted temporarily with poppets at the bow and the stern, which stabilized the ship and directed its motion as it slid down the ways and entered the water. (NARA, all)

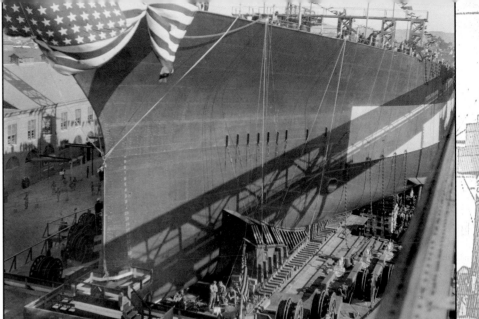

Above left: The *California* is nearly ready for launching, with flag bunting suspended from the bow. On the platform alongside the hull is a row of reels that fed cables through brakes to the ship. As the ship made its way down the ways upon launching, these cables would act to reduce the ship's velocity so that, if all went by plan, it would come to a stop in the middle of the Napa River channel. (Vallejo Naval and Historical Museum) **Top right:** The left side of the bow poppet is in view, secured by cables to fittings on the hull.

To the lower right are the left brake-cable drums. The two-inch wire cables were fed from the drums into the brakes, and then to five leader chains on each side, fastened to the hull. (NARA) **Above right:** On launching day, 20 November 1919, members of the launching party stand by the brake-cable drums along *California's* port bow. To the rear of each set of drums is a shield made of wooden planks through which the cables made their ways to the brakes. (Mare Island Museum)

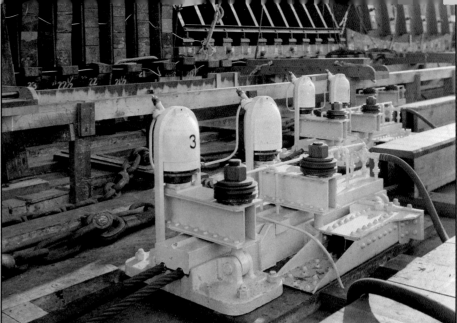

5208 - U. S. S. CALIFORNIA.

Top left: Cable drums and the wooden cable shields off the starboard bow are shown. To the far left is one of the brakes. Also in view is the right side of the bow poppet, its cable moorings to the hull, and details of the packing and cradle supporting the hull. **Top right:** Two of the brakes to the starboard side of *California*'s hull are viewed. To slow down the ship, hydraulic pressure was applied to two metal blocks, which squeezed the two cables running through each brake. Two leader chains shackled to the cables are at the left. **Above left:** The brakes were charged by manually operated hydraulic pumps on each

side of *California*'s bow. Before the ship was launched on 20 November 1919, these men pumped sufficient hydraulic pressure to provide 850 psi to each set of brakes. **Above right:** The packing and shoring supporting the after part of the *California* prior to launching is observed from the starboard side facing forward. The poppet at the center has been cut out to provide clearance to the inboard propeller shaft. A bilge keel is to the far right. (NARA)

In a general view of the bow of the *California* before the launching, the four starboard brake-cable reels and brakes are in view. In the foreground is the starboard hydraulic pump stand by which the brakes were powered. The poppets and wooden shoring referred to as packing supported the massive weight of the ship and were carefully designed to conform to the contours of the hull. The poppets and the packing slid down the greased slipway along with the hull when it was launched. (NARA)

The *California* is christened

The hull of the *California* was scheduled for launching at 11:45 AM on 20 November 1919, 1,121 days after her keel was laid. Standing on the launching platform were *California*'s sponsor, Barbara Stephens Zane, daughter of Golden State governor William Stephens, and Mare Island Commandant Captain Edward Beach (father of the noted author of the same name).

Beach triggered the launch, and Mrs. Zane simultaneously swung the bottle of champagne, declaring, "I christen thee *California*." Almost immediately thereafter things began to go awry. *California*, taking to the water at a speed greater than 15 miles per hour, strained against the ten reels of braking cables, held to her bow with heavy chains. One by one the chains parted as the huge hull, propelled by gravity and inertia, moved across the Mare Island Channel, intent it seemed, in finding a new birth in the middle of Georgia street, in downtown Vallejo.

Yard workers, numbering 300, were aboard, and scrambled to deploy their last-ditch arresting gear. Heavy manila lines were cut, dropping two emergency anchors, one on each side of the bow, to the bottom of the muddy channel. The anchors began to dig in, and they, along with the heavy timber pilings of the Vallejo ferry pier, brought *California*'s immense hull to a stop.

Eight tugboats extricated *California* in short order, $1,500 repaired the ferry pier, and an extensive investigation was launched as to why the cable arresting gear, a system used previously with other vessels, failed to perform in this case.

Above left: The launching preparations, christening, and actual launching of the *California* were intensively documented by still and movie cameramen. This photo of the hull dressed-out with flags from stem to stern was taken from the Napa River, with the colonnaded façade of the ferry house to the right. The propellers were not installed yet but would be mounted during the post-launching fitting out. "CALIFORNIA" was in raised letters on each side of the stern just below the main deck. (Vallejo Naval and Historical Museum) **Above right:** The after packing below the *California* is viewed from the port side on around the launching date. The port outboard propeller shaft and struts are visible; the inboard port propeller shaft is hidden behind the stern poppet. The thin fin at the top is a bilge keel. (NARA)

Top left The sponsor of the *California*, who christened the ship upon launching, was Mrs. Barbara Stephens Zane, daughter of Gov. William Stephens of California. Mrs. Zane is seen here with her daughter, Marjorie Zane, maid of honor at the christening, on launching day. (NARA) **Above left:** Mrs. Barbara Stephens Zane poses with the commandant of the Mare Island Navy Yard, Capt. Edward R. Beach, on launching day, 20 November 1919.

Mrs. Zane is wearing a medal featuring an image of the bear that is symbolic of the State of California. (Mare Island Museum) **Above right:** Mrs. Zane prepares to smash the ceremonial bottle on the bow of the *California*. Although the beginning of Prohibition was two months away and there was much anti-alcohol sentiment at the time, California wine was used as the christening liquid. (NARA)

Left: Mrs. Zane has just smashed the wine bottle on the bow of *California*, thus christening the ship. Behind her, a navy bugler blows. On the guard rail around the christening platform is a placard with crossed riveting hammers: a time-honored symbol of ironworks and shipyards, and these hammers may have been those used to drive the first rivets in the keel. An instant before the christening, two triggers had been actuated, which released the ship from its tethers, putting it in motion. (NARA) **Top right:** The christening of the ship was at 11:45 a.m. on 20 November 1919. To get to this point required a carefully orchestrated schedule, including greasing the ways, testing and setting the brakes, and removing shores and building blocks one at a time. (NARA) **Above right:** In a photo

off the starboard stern of the California shortly before she was launched, it is evident just how close the ship was to the ferry house (right). The rudder has been immobilized by an H-shaped lock wedged between the stern and the top of the rudder. This was to prevent the rudder from moving and being damaged when the ship entered and was gliding through the water upon launching. Draft numbers on the stern were a light color up to the waterline and a dark color above the waterline. (NARA)

5340 - U.S.S. CALIFORNIA, LAUNCHING.
MARE ISLAND CAL. NOV 20 1920

Top left: Holding a bouquet, Mrs. Vane, on the left side of the christening platform, waves as the *California* gains momentum on its trip down the slipway. From this angle, the bulbous bow is visible. This feature enhanced the performance and handling of the ship. (NARA) **Above left:** The ship sliding down the ways is viewed from another angle. On the ship were various work parties with specific tasks to perform during the launching, such as tending chronographs, taking soundings, and observing for problems in-

side and on deck. (Mare Island Museum) **Above right:** The *California* has slid into the Napa River, and it is apparent from this angle just how close the opposite shore and downtown Vallejo are. Long before the launching, engineers had worked on the problem of launching such a massive ship so that it would come to a stop in mid-channel: a real challenge, since the ship was 624 feet long, and the channel was less than twice that wide, at 1,230 feet. (NARA)

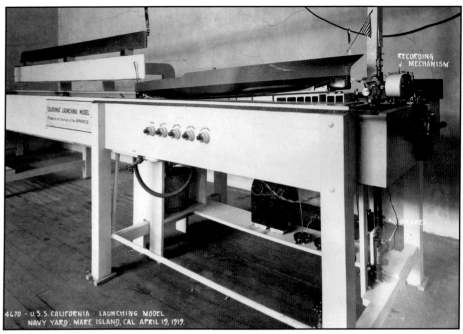

4670 - U.S.S. CALIFORNIA LAUNCHING MODEL
NAVY YARD, MARE ISLAND, CAL. APRIL 19, 1919.

CALIFORNIA LAUNCHING MODEL

RECORDING MECHANISM

BRAKES

Top left: The U.S. flag whipping smartly from a staff on the stern, the *California* has cleared the slipway, as viewed from the waterfront in Vallejo. An anchor on each side well aft of the bow was dropped in an attempt to slow her motion, but they took time to dig in. (NARA) **Top right:** More than a half-year before the launching of *California*, this scale model of the hull and the slipway was constructed to simulate the launching. To the left is a water trough simulating the Napa River channel, and to the right is a mechanism for recording data. (Mare Island Museum) **Above:** The theory of the scale model and engineering plans for the launching were put to the test on 20 November 1919. Here, as viewed from downstream near the eastern shore of the river, the stern of *California* plows into the water while the bow is still on the slipway. (Mare Island Museum)

Top: Just how little space there was in the Napa River for a ship of *California*'s size to be launched is evident in this photo. Despite efforts to arrest her momentum, the ship was more than halfway across the river, and it appeared that she might crash ashore. (Mare Island Museum) **Above left:** After several tense moments, the *California* finally came to rest, but not before striking and damaging some pilings and part of the Mare Island Ferry slip. The twin-towered ferry house next to the *California*'s slipway is across the river to the right of the ship. **Above right:** One of the many photographers present on the day of the launching captured this close-up of the stern of *California* while mired among the pilings of the ferry slip. Mud on the river bottom was the factor that finally had brought the ship to a stop in the nick of time. (NARA, both)

Top left: Eventually on launching day, tugboats came alongside the *California*, pried her loose from the mud, and maneuvered her to her fitting-out dock. At the bottom of the stern is a massive wooden lock for the rudder to prevent it from turning during launching. (NARA) **Top right:** Tugboats of the Red Stack Tug Company push the *California* away from the east shore. Fortunately, the embarrassing episode at the Mare Island Ferry slip had not caused damage to the ship. To the left is the slipway from which the ship had been launched. (Mare Island Museum) **Above left:** Tugboats are easing the *California* toward the Mare Island shore. Although other ships would be built and launched at Mare Island Navy Yard, the *California* was the only battleship ever produced there. The channel was simply too narrow for capital ships. (NARA) **Above right:**

California is en route to her fitting-out dock on 20 November 1919. After a rough launching, the ship would now settle in for months of further construction, which would include the installation of above-decks structures and equipment and interior finishing. (NARA)

Top left: From the time of *California*'s launching in late November 1919 until her commissioning almost two years later, on 10 August 1921, the ship underwent fitting-out at Mare Island. This view taken on 2 January 1920 looks forward from amidships to the upper deck. (NARA) **Top right:** During February 1920, 150-ton floating crane YD-33 lies alongside the *California*. This big crane placed large components on the battleship's deck, and the temporary derrick on the ship then moved the items where needed. A canvas sun cover is over the fantail. (Mare Island Museum) **Above left:** In a photo taken off the starboard bow, the conning tower and, aft of it, the superstructure are under construction. To the front of the conning tower is the tall barbette for turret two. The belt armor has been installed; it is the dark area along the side of the hull. (Mare Island Museum) **Above right:** The live ring is being lowered into its seating in the barbette of turret number one. This ring bore the rollers upon which the turret would rotate within the barbette. In the background are the barbette of turret number two and the front of the conning tower. (NARA)

Above left: One of the 14-inch gun turrets for the *California*, sans gun house enclosure, is being readied for installation on the ship, and lines are rigged from the structure to a sling with dual four-sheave blocks on top, operated by the floating crane to the far left. The two men look down into the well of the left gun. The front of the turret is to the left. The turrets were placed on their barbettes in the spring of 1920. **Above right:** Floating Crane YD-33 hoists turret two for installation in its barbette on the *California*. Some naval and civilian officials stand on the rim of the barbette and the wooden scaffolding by the barbette. The top of the barbette that will form the foundation for turret number one is to the far right. To the left is the conning tower, which will be the command and control center of the ship during battle.

Above left: The boom of YD-33 is lowering turret number two into its barbette, with several feet left to go before it will be firmly seated. The three 14-inch guns later will be mounted between the tilted girders of the turret, and the interior of the turret will be constructed, topped off by the armored gun-house enclosure. The turret officer's station will occupy the rear overhang of the turret. **Top right:** On 2 August 1920 the construction of the gun houses of turrets one and two is underway at Mare Island. The sides, glacis (front plate), and roof are present on turret one, while the sides and roof beams are visible on turret two. Reels of wire are on the foredeck. (Mare Island Museum) **Above right:** *California* is viewed from astern on 2 August 1920. In the shadows along the hull is the belt armor. Internal framing of turret three is visible aft of the superstructure. Openings for two 5-inch gun casemates are visible above the first gangplank to the right. (NARA)

Top left: In a 2 August 1921 view aft from the bridge, workmen are constructing the aft smokestack. Farther aft is the interior framework of turret three. The turret is flanked by several deck ventilators with angular hoods, some of which lack their tops. **Top right:** A floating crane is lowering the mainmast in place on 10 September 1920. The masts were the "cage" type, with criss-crossing pipes clamped together where they intersected to form a strong structure that was less vulnerable to a direct hit than a solid structure. **Above left:** The progress of work on the forward part of *California* is documented in this

27 September 1920 view. Numerous primer touchups had been performed preparatory to repainting the ship. To the right is a stiff-leg crane used for heavy-lifting operations at the dock. **Above right:** Four days after the preceding photo was taken, the *California* sports a fresh paint job. The ship now has a black boot topping along the future water-line; this was a plastic-based coating that masked the oil that tended to adhere to the hull of a ship when in port. (NARA, all)

Top left: On 29 November 1920 the *California* was towed from Mare Island to the Bethlehem Shipbuilding Corp. dry dock at Hunters Point, San Francisco, for removal of the remnants of the launching cradle from the hull. Here, the ship is just departing from Mare Island. **Top right:** An aerial view captured the *California* under tow as it rounds the point of Mare Island, with Vallejo in the distance, during the trip to Hunters Point on 29 November 1920. The ship stopped that evening at California City and completed the trip the next day. **Above left:** The *California* is viewed off her port bow while being towed to Hunters Point on 29 November 1920. Temporary covers were over the gun ports of the turrets. Scaffolding was still around the cage masts; the ship was still very much a work in progress. **Above right:** On 20 November 1920 the *California* enters a dry dock at Hunters Point Shipyard. In addition to removing the remaining launching packing from the lower part of the hull, another purpose for the dry-docking was to in-spect the sea-water inlet ports. (Mare Island Museum, all)

On the *California* poised in dry dock at Hunters Point, standing tall on the outboard side of the superstructure is the kingpost for the port boat derrick. In the control top on each cage mast, the upper story was primary-battery control, from which the 14-inch guns would be controlled, and the lower story was secondary-battery control, from which the 5-inch battery would be directed. The primary-battery control on each mast lacked its roof at this time. (Mare Island Museum)

Above left: During *California's* dry-docking at Hunters Point on 1 December 1920, workmen are scraping the hull from the boot topping down to remove marine growth. At this point the ship was equipped with two anchors, housed in the center and the starboard hawse pipes. **Above right:** In a view of the *California* from astern in dry dock, the packing, or cribbing, that was installed to support the overhanging stern for launch-ing is seen around the inboard propeller shaft. Removing this packing was the principal reason for this dry-docking, and it took a crew of 130 riggers and mechanics to extricate the structures. The propellers were not installed during this period in dry dock at Hunters Point but were emplaced after the ship was commissioned. (NARA, both)

By 5 January 1921, when this photograph was taken, the *California* had been towed back to Mare Island Navy Yard for further fitting-out. A floating crane has come alongside the starboard beam of the ship, and a trolley crane on the dock is available for heavy lifting. (NARA)

6260 - U.S.S. CALIFORNIA, MARE ISLAND, CAL JAN 5, 1921.

6380 - U.S.S. CALIFORNIA, MARE ISLAND CAL. APRIL 2, 1921.

Top left: The *California* is visible in the background through shipyard equipment on 30 March 1921. All three anchors are now installed, and the operation of mounting the 14-inch/50-caliber guns has begun. Turret two, traversed to port, displays at least one 14-inch gun. (Naval History and Heritage Command) **Above left:** Turret number two is the centerpiece of this photo probably taken in late March or April 1921. The floating crane out of the view to the left is hoisting the right 14-inch gun into the gun house through the open rear of the structure. To the lower left is turret one. (Mare Island Museum) **Above right:** The status of work on fitting out the *California* is documented in this frontal view dated 2 April 1921. The bulwark of the bridge on the conning tower is completed or nearly so. Recesses for the rangefinder are in the upper rear of the sides of turrets one and two. The armored belt extending above the waterline (and well below it as well) is visible on each side of the hull.

6385- U.S.S. CALIFORNIA,
OKING FORD FROM AFTER MAST.
MARE ISLAND, CAL. APRIL 2, 1921.

6384- U. S. S. CALIFORNIA,
MARE ISLAND, CAL. APRIL 2, 1921.

Above left: By 1 April 1921, when this photo was taken from the control top of the main-mast, all three 14-inch guns had been installed in turret two of *California*, and they are in view turned to port. At the bottom is the forward smokestack, with a fabric cover fitted over the top. The poles jutting from the forward control top were temporary installations for rigging safety lines. **Above right:** *California* is viewed from aft of her fantail in a photo dated 2 April 1921. The gun house for turret four has its sides but no glacis or roof. Visible inside the turret are the three sleeves in which the 14-inch guns would be mounted, providing a recoil enclosure for them. The turret-three gun house has its glacis, an 18-inch-thick slab of armor. The 14-inch guns have yet to be installed. (NARA, both)

C457 - U.S.S. CALIFORNIA,
MARE ISLAND CAL. JUNE 1, 1921.
LOOKING AFT.

Above left: In a view from the rear of the forward control top facing aft on 1 June 1921, the top of the forward smokestack is partially visible toward the bottom, the aft smokestack is at the center of the photo, and the mainmast is at the top. A searchlight platform is on the mainmast. To the lower right are two gun mounts on the superstructure deck, including a 5-inch/51-caliber with a splinter shield. (NARA) **Top right:** In a photo taken around June 1921, the 14-inch guns of turret number one, not present in the 2

April 1921 photographs, are now present. The layout of the anchor chains is evident. (Mare Island Museum) **Top left:** The *California* is viewed from off the port stern at around the same time the preceding photo was taken. All of the 14-inch guns are now mounted in turrets three and four. Also, the 5-inch/51-caliber guns are mounted in the casemates along the upper deck, and the control tops appear to be completed, with the yardarms installed on them. (Mare Island Museum)

G480 - U.S.S. CALIFORNIA
MARE ISLAND, CAL. JULY I, 1921.

G482 - U.S.S. CALIFORNIA.
MARE ISLAND, CAL. JULY, I, 1921.

Above left: With a little more than a month to go before the ship is commissioned, fitting-out work proceeds on the *California* at Mare Island on 1 July 1921. Atop the navigating bridge or pilot house is a rangefinder that had been mounted earlier in the year; it is traversed to port. This rangefinder served the main battery. The masts and yardarms were now fully rigged. **Above right:** On the same date the preceding photo was taken, this image was recorded at a higher angle, showing details of the foredeck. At the point of the bow is the jackstaff. The anchor chains run from the anchors in the hawse pipes back to the windlasses. Short lengths of chain called stoppers are fastened to the deck and to the anchor chains near the hawse pipes. (NARA, both)

Top left: Officers and crew are assembled on the quarterdeck of the *California* on 10 August 1921 for the commissioning ceremony. This marked the placement of the ship into active service with the U.S. Navy and the formal transfer of the ship to its commanding officer. (Mare Island Museum) **Top right:** Captain Henry J. Ziegemeier, right, the first commanding officer of the USS *California* (BB-44), addresses the assembled officers, crew, and dignitaries at the commissioning ceremony. Third from left is Capt. Edward L. Beach Sr., commandant of the shipyard. (Mare Island Museum)

Above left: The *California* is viewed from astern during the commissioning ceremony on 10 August 1921. The port boat boom is extended, and several barges are moored to it. Another boat boom was on the opposite side, secured in its stowed position against the hull. (NARA) **Above right:** Although the quarterdeck of USS *California* was cleared and ship-shape for the commissioning ceremony, the rest of the ship was still an active work zone. Large frames, the purpose of which is unclear, were temporarily installed forward and aft. (Mare Island Museum)

Top left: The commissioning crew, also known as the plank owners, poses on the *California* using every available space. In the foreground are several ship's mascots: only the light-colored goat, "Billy Vallejo," is readily discerned; also present were a dog and a cub bear. **Top right:** Captain Henry J. Ziegemeier, first captain of the *California*, sits in front of his roll-top desk in his handsomely appointed cabin. **Above left:** In 1908 the citizens of San Diego presented the armored cruiser *California* with a carved onyx punch set with gold bands around the bowl and the goblets. The battleship *California* inherited that set, seen here, after the cruiser was renamed *San Diego*. **Above right:** The *California*'s punch set and silver service are grouped together. The silver service, too, was presented originally to the armored cruiser *California*. In 1974 both the silver service and the punch set were presented to the nuclear guided missile cruiser *California*. (Mare Island Museum, all)

A few days after the commissioning, USS *California* was towed once again to dry dock at Hunters Point, this time for installation of the four propellers, hull painting, and inclining tests. Bluejackets stand by as the ship enters the dry dock on 22 August. (Mare Island Museum)

Five days after the preceding photo was taken, the *California* is undergoing work in the dry dock. The hull below the waterline is in rough shape after almost two years in the water, and the repainting of the hull below the waterline would soon begin. (Mare Island Museum)

Vapor rises from the smokestacks of the *California* in dry dock on 6 September 1921. The hull below the boot topping has received fresh paint, and a few workmen on staging planks are performing finishing touches. All four propellers now were mounted. (Mare Island Museum)

The crew lines the rails as USS *California* departs from San Francisco Bay in mid-September 1921. During this first foray to sea, the ship would perform acceptance trials, testing its performance and making sure all systems were ready for active operations. On the rear of the main mast is a range clock. Rather than a timepiece, this was a visual indicator of the range of a designated target. Using the visual references of the concentration dial and the azimuth scales painted on turrets two and three, fire-controllers in other ships in the battle line could lay their big guns on the same target. (Mare Island Museum)

Top: California underwent several trials testing systems and evaluating performance during September and October 1921. Here she makes 21 knots steaming east during speed run number 18, her clipper bow pushing back a heavy bow wave. (Mare Island Museum) **Above:** During one of her early runs, the *California* steams past Alcatraz Island and its famed penitentiary in San Francisco Bay. A full complement of motor whale boats and barges is stacked on the deck abeam the smokestacks, and another boat is suspended from davits. (Mare Island Museum, both)

Above left: In one of the fire rooms of the *California*, two crewmen make adjustments to valves to regulate burners in a photograph dated 6 September 1921. The eight Bureau Express boilers generated steam to drive the General Electric turbogenerators. (Mare Island Museum) **Top right:** One of USS *California*'s generators is depicted in a 6 September 1921 photo. There were two turbogenerator rooms, each having one turbine and two generators to power the motors, and three ship's service generators to provide electricity to the ship. (NARA) **Above right:** As built, USS *California* had five casemates on each side of the foredeck with 5-inch/51-caliber secondary-battery guns. Shown here in a 1 October 1921 photo is one of the casemate gun crews, also displaying two shells and one bagged powder charge. (Mare Island Museum)

The *California* was photographed from a passing aircraft in San Francisco Bay around 1922. The azimuth scales painted on turrets two and three are quite visible. Light-colored canvas covers are over the openings of the casemates on the foredeck level. (NARA)

Top left: By 1923, USS *California* had at least one scout plane assigned to it: a Vought UO-1 two-seater biplane. This plane's U.S. Navy Bureau Number, A-6603, was marked at the top of the rudder. The UO-1 could be fitted with landing gear, as seen here, or with floats. (National Museum of Naval Aviation) **Top right:** By October 1923 a catapult for launching scout planes had been installed on the fantail of USS *California*. Here, several officers and sailors pose in front of the catapult, mounted upon which is a Vought UO-1 scout plane with a center float and wing floats. (Mare Island Museum) **Above left:**

The recently installed catapult is visible in the background of this photo taken from the starboard aft corner of the 01 level of the *California* in 1923. In the foreground are two of the ship's 3-inch/50-caliber antiaircraft guns. The band is playing on the quarterdeck. (National Park Service) **Above right:** One of the *California*'s Vought UO-1 scout planes competed in the 1923 St. Louis International Air Races in early October 1923. An unidentified officer and a civilian stand by the plane; on the wing is a hand-lettered informational placard about the UO-1. (National Museum of Naval Aviation)

Top left: USS *California* transits the Panama Canal for the first time. The ship passed through the canal in January 1924 en route to New York and again that April on the return trip to California. A UO-1 is on the catapult in this view taken in the Gatun Locks. (Mare Island Museum) **Top right:** On 24 February 1924 during battle exercises, one of USS *California*'s Vought UO-1 scout planes, USN bureau number A-6603, is heading for a crash upon launching. The plane was badly damaged in the crash landing, and the *California* recovered the wreck. (National Park Service)

Above left: Following her participation in fleet problems in the Caribbean in early 1924, the *California* visited New York City in early March. The battleship is seen against the Manhattan skyline. Substantial covers are installed over the 14-inch gun muzzles. (National Park Service) **Above right:** The azimuth scale painted on the side of turret three is clearly shown in this view of sailors swabbing the decks as *California* steams in formation. Although a catapult is not visible on the fantail, an aircraft hoist boom is clearly seen. (National Park Service)

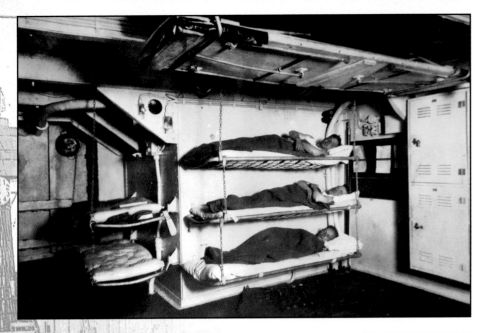

Top left: Hammocks had been a time-honored means of berthing sailors in U.S. Navy ships, but in August 1924 during a refitting at Navy Yard Puget Sound in Bremerton, Washington, folding bunks were installed in various compartments. *California* was the first battleship to be so equipped, as part of an experiment. (National Park Service) **Top right:** Floodlights illuminate the fantail of USS *California* on the night of 26 November 1924 as Lt. Dixie Kiefer in a Vought UO-1 A-6494, Bureau Number A-6494, prepares to make the first nighttime catapult launching of an aircraft from a battleship. The launching and flight were successful. (National Park Service) **Above left:** Despite the steel-and-rivets ambience, the captain's cabin of USS *California* had touches of elegance and comfort, such as leather-upholstered furniture, a sideboard and china cabinet, Persian throw rugs, and a centerpiece and tablecloth on the dining table. (NARA) **Above right:** A sailor explains the workings of a 21-inch torpedo to a group of civilians on the foredeck of USS *California*. This image also provides a clear view of the three wildcats, the rotating heads of the windlasses that were molded to fit the anchor chains. (National Park Service)

In an aerial view of the *California* dated 5 April 1925, two of the ship's scout planes are stored in tandem on the catapult. Another scout plane, apparently partially disassembled, is stowed adjacent to the superstructure to the rear of the ship's boats. (NARA via Roger Torgeson)

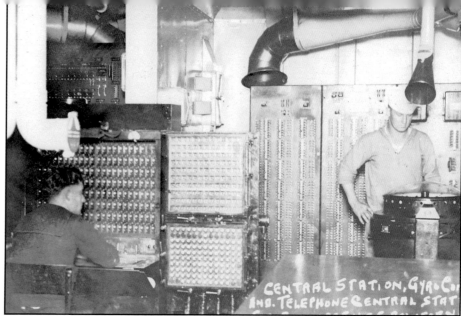

Top left: USS *California* was photographed at sea from a plane from Naval Air Station Pearl Harbor on 30 April 1925. The battleship was part of a Blue Fleet of 127 ships that had sailed from San Francisco to engage in war games in the Hawaiian Islands. (NARA)

Top right: In central station on the *California* in a 1925 photograph, to the left is an operator on the ship's central telephone switchboard. To the right, a sailor monitors the gyrocompass. The gyrocompass was an important adjunct to the ship's magnetic compasses. (San Diego Air and Space Museum) **Above left:** USS *California's* Vought UO-1 number 1, Bureau Number A-7004, is poised on the catapult on the fantail in an undated photo from the 1920s. The catapult is trained to port, with the barrels of the 14-inch/50-caliber guns of turret number four appearing in the foreground. (San Diego Air and Space Museum) **Above right:** Two of *California's* Vought UO-1 scout planes are on the catapult facing aft. The forward plane is marked number "1," while the aft plane is marked number 2. Subcaliber guns for target practice are on the center 14-inch guns of turrets three and four. (National Park Service)

The *California* is anchored in Hawaiian territorial waters on 3 May 1925. In the distance are several ships of the fleet. During May 1925 the *California* largely operated between Maui and Oahu, frequently lying at anchor off Lahaina, Maui, and Honolulu, Oahu.

This aerial photograph of USS *California* in Hawaiian waters was taken on 6 May 1925 from an altitude of 1,300 feet. One of her observation planes is stored to the port side of the catapult, and another one is visible to the port side of the mainmast. (NARA via Roger Torgeson)

Top left: Submarine chaser SC-306 and several ship's barges are alongside the stern of USS *California*. The Vought UO-1 toward the top is on the catapult, while the other UO-1 is on a dolly with a mechanism to raise the aircraft in line with the top of the catapult. (National Park Service) **Top right:** In a photograph taken from *California*'s maintop on the same occasion as the preceding photo, a mixed crowd of sailors and civilians watches as a Vought UO-1 prepares for launching to starboard from the catapult on the fantail. (National Park Service) **Above left:** A Vought UO-1 assigned to USS

California rests on a dolly on a hardstand at North Island, San Diego, California, sometime during 1926. This aircraft was USN Bureau Number A-6861 and was marked with the number 2 under "CALIFORNIA." (San Diego Air and Space Museum) **Above right:** The original caption of this post card read, "Sunday on the forecastle of USS *California*." A clear view is available of the gun shield of the 5-inch gun on the 01 level, to the rear of which are stacked boats. (National Park Service)

S-CLASS SUBMARINES

2 V-CLASS SUBMARINES

2 S-CLASS SUBMARINES

In an aerial photo taken over the New York (or Brooklyn) Navy Yard on 2 May 1927, USS *California* is the large ship toward the bottom. By now, a second catapult had been installed, atop turret three, and a rangefinder was atop the conning tower. (NARA via Roger Torgeson)

SUBMARINE TENDER "CAMDEN"

BATTLESHIP MARYLAND

BATTLESHIP CALIFORNIA

3 - 1200 TON DESTROYERS

The *California* at sea sometime between September 1927 and June 1928. At the time, the Navy believed each battleship should carry three types of aircraft, and *California* (as ComBatFlt) was included. Squadron VO-1 provided a Loening OL amphibia—the large aircraft seen on the high catapult. Squadron VO-2 provided a Vought UO observation aircraft, and squadron VF-2 provided a Vought FU-1 (the single-seat fighter version of the UO).

At first, the two observation types carried the same individual code number: 1/10 for the OL and 2/10 for the UO. The fighter was initially coded 2-F-1 (with the squadron commander stationed aboard the flagship), but in January 1928 the aircraft was recoded as 2-F-10. That meant that in the Pacific for about six months, any battleship aircraft with the #10 was from *California*.

Of course, in retrospect, the Navy plan was foolish. Three aircrews from three squadrons caused chain-of-command nightmares. Three different aircraft and engines created spare parts and maintenance nightmares. The mixed squadron/mission experiment ended in June 1928, when all aircraft were removed from all battleships. (NARA)

Top left: A Loening OL-4 with markings for USS *California* is being hoisted aboard around 1930. This plane had retractable landing gear, shown extended in this image. Only six Loening OL-4s were produced: U.S. Navy Bureau Numbers A-7059 to A-7064. (San Diego Air and Space Museum) **Above left:** In a view of sailors crowded on the aft 14-inch turrets of *California*, at the top is the underside of the catapult on turret three. Mounted on the catapult is a Loening OL scout plane. Projecting from turret four at the center is the left side of the rangefinder. (San Diego Air and Space Museum) **Above right:** A Loening OL scout plane is mounted on the high catapult on turret number three on USS *California* as the ship passes through the Gatun Locks in the Panama Canal around the late 1920s. Three more scout planes are visible on the ship: one on the fantail catapult, one adjacent to the fantail catapult, and one stored laterally on the quarterdeck to the port side of turret four. (LOC)

Top: USS *California* is docked at Balboa, Canal Zone, during one of the periodic fleet concentrations. The ship is decked out in full dress, with national ensigns flying from the masts and flags and pennants streaming from lines from stem to stern. **Above:** A Loening OL scout plane is on the catapult atop turret number three in this undated photograph of USS *California* lying off a mountainous coastline. The rangefinder atop the conning tower, which had been installed by May 1927, is clearly visible. (NARA, both)

Top left: The secondary-battery crews of USS *California* fire the 5-inch/51-caliber guns during night battle practice off San Pedro, California, around 1927. One of the 5-inch guns on the forward starboard corner of the 01 level, at the center of the photo, has just fired. (NARA) **Top right:** In January 1928, USS *California* was in dry dock at Hunters Point, San Francisco, California. Staging planks are suspended from lines along the hull for work parties, who appear to be renewing the boot topping, the black band along the waterline. (National Park Service) **Above left:** Vought O2U-3 Corsairs of Observation Squadron 4 (VO-4) are on the turret-three catapult and the fantail catapult of *California* sometime between 4 Dec 1928 and 1 April 1931. The plane on the turret-three catapult is marked "4/11" on the side of the fuselage. (NARA) **Above right:** Gunnery practice is underway on the *California*. Turret one is trained to port preparatory to firing a broadside. The secondary battery of 5-inch guns amidships has unloosed a volley. Those guns were intended to contend with midsized threats such as destroyers. (National Park Service)

3" AIR CRAFT GUN
U.S.S. CALIFORNIA

Top left: The *California* is moored to a dock at an unidentified sometime between January 1928 and May 1932, during which time a bulwark on the bridge around the upper level of the conning tower was removed. In this photo, the bulwark has been replaced by rails. (San Diego Air and Space Museum) **Above left:** An officer walks past one of USS *California*'s 3-inch/50-caliber antiaircraft guns. On top of the barrel is a sub-caliber gun used during target practice to save on ammunition costs. (San Diego Air and Space Museum) **Above right:** One of the *California*'s 3-inch/50-caliber antiaircraft guns is set at full elevation. The pointer and the trainer, who elevated and traversed the mount, stood on small platforms and utilized the dual hand wheels and sights. Operating the gun at such high elevation put a real strain on the gun operators. (Author's collection)

Top: USS *California* rests at anchor in San Francisco Bay in May 1932. Boarding ladders are emplaced on the side of the hull and a boat boom is extended to which small craft can be moored. In port, the national ensign is flown from the flagstaff on the stern. (San Diego Air and Space Museum) **Above left:** A boatful of children approaches USS *California* anchored in San Francisco Bay in May 1932. Marked on the fuselage of the Vought

O3U on the turret-three catapult is "BATTLE FORCE," the title at that time of the Pacific element of the U.S. Fleet. (San Diego Air and Space Museum) **Above right:** A crew serves one of USS *California*'s 5-inch/25-caliber guns. The ship's original antiaircraft battery of 3-inch/50-caliber guns was replaced during a 1929-1930 refitting by eight 5-inch/25-caliber guns. They were located on the 01 level. (NARA)

Top left: Naval ships sometimes had to dispatch landing parties to act as infantry ashore. Here, a sailor poses with a display of landing force equipment, including rifles, a bedroll, and assorted equipment, below the 14-inch guns of one of USS *California's* turrets. (National Park Service) **Top right:** The Battle Force, including USS *California*, participated in Fleet Problem XV in the Caribbean in spring 1934, after which the force proceeded to New York for review by President Franklin D. Roosevelt. The *California's* crew lines the rails for the 31 May review. (NARA) **Above:** The *California* was photographed from another angle on 31 May 1934. The Navy Blue mainmast was a feature of the *California* from 1931 to 1935. The blue part of the cage mast extended from above the searchlight control platform to below the fighting top. (NARA)

This aerial photo of USS *California* apparently was taken on the occasion of the presidential review off New York on 31 May 1934, with the crew lining the rails and the ship exhibiting the same assortment of scout planes on the catapults and deck. (San Diego Air and Space Museum)

Top left: A close-up of the preceding photograph shows the three observation planes on the *California* on 31 May 1934. On the catapult on turret three is the Vought O3U-3 assigned to the Commander, Battle Force. On the fantail are two Vought O3U-3s. (San Diego Air and Space Museum) **Top right:** It was probably at the time of USS *California's* visit to New York City in spring 1934 that this photo of the ship cruising past the Manhattan skyline was taken. Still on the high catapult is the dark-fuselage Vought O3U-3 marked for the commander, Battle Force. (NARA) **Above:** The *California* is anchored in the Hudson River off Manhattan on 16 June 1934. The Vought O3U-3 on the rear of the catapult has the fuselage code 3-O-15, signifying Observation Squadron 3, while the O3U-3 to the front of it has no fuselage code. (Author's collection)

USS *California* is anchored off San Pedro, California, in an undated photograph. To the far right is the Angel's Gate Lighthouse. The searchlight-control platform on the main-mast, removed around 1936, is still present, visible behind the boat crane. To the sides of the superstructure are the boat cranes. (NARA)

Top: When this photo of the *California* was taken on 23 August 1935, the upper portion of the mainmast still was painted Navy Blue. The only aircraft visible onboard is the Vought O3U-3 with the dark fuselage assigned to Commander, Battle Force. (NARA)
Above: USS *California* is seen from the air in another 23 August 1935 photograph. By now, the shields that long had been mounted on the 5-inch guns on each side of the front of the 01 level had been removed. Notably, by this time platforms with 50-cal machine guns had added to the Fighting Tops. The raised boarding ladders cast shadows against the hull. (NARA via Rick Davis)

The *California* is anchored in a harbor, the 14-inch guns of turret number one trained to port. Two sailors sitting on a plank are touching up the paint between the bow and turret one. The searchlight-control platform is gone, dating this photo to 1936 or after. (NARA)

USS *California* periodically visited San Pedro, California, in the decades before the Pearl Harbor attack. The battleship is seen at anchor there sometime in or before the mid-1930s. Anchored in the left background is a battleship with tripod masts. (NARA)

California is viewed from ahead off San Pedro sometime before mid-1935. By that time, tubs had been installed to each side of the searchlight bridge on front of the conning tower. A bulwark around that bridge present in 1920s photos was removed by 1932. (NARA)

California steams across San Francisco Bay around the fall of 1936 with the two spans of the newly built San Francisco-Oakland Bay Bridge and Angel Island in the background. Four observation planes are aboard. (NARA)

USS *California* (BB44) 1936

California as she was fitted in 1936 included catapults on the
fantail and atop turret three. The two funnels of the original
design are readily apparent midships.

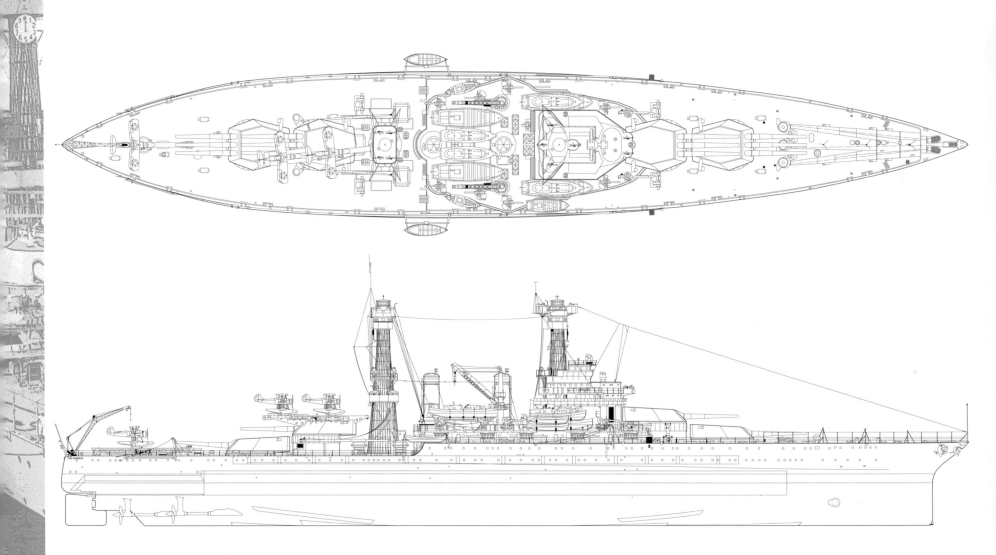

In a photo very likely related to the preceding two, USS *California* is viewed from above. During a recent modernization, the searchlight-control platform below the searchlight platform on the mainmast had been removed. The number 44 is faintly visible atop turret two. (National Park Service)

In a photo taken at an unidentified port between August 1934 and June 1937, the two scout planes on the fantail of *California* are marked on the fuselage 4-O-11 and 4-O-12. The previous practice of placing a slash mark after the squadron number was discontinued in 1930. (NARA)

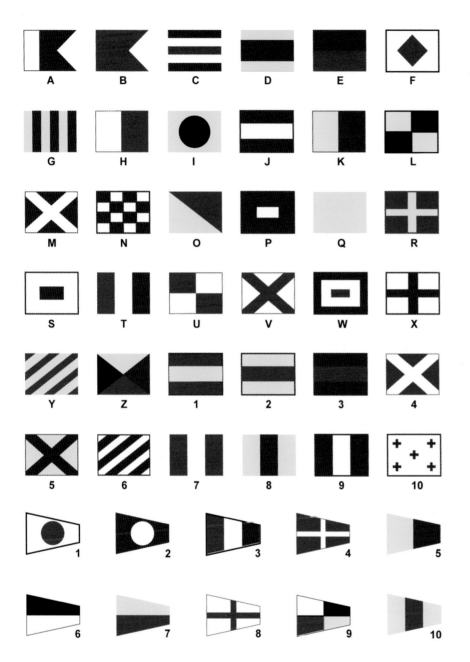

Above: These signal flags were and are used to communicate without use of radio equipment. In addition to the individual letter or number associated with each flag, within the US Navy each flag has an individual meaning; for instance, the "J" flag, which means "I am on fire and have dangerous cargo, keep clear." **Right:** As seen from the forecastle of USS *California* probably in the 1930s, the ship is fully dressed for a holiday or special occasion. When fully dressed, the national ensign was flown from the flagstaff and each masthead, and flags were hung from lines from bow to stern. (NARA)

The Pearl Harbor Attack

"...0803 ships of the U.S. Pacific Fleet opened fire on attacking planes. Opened fire with 50 caliber machine guns #1 and #2 at one torpedo plane. 0805 struck with one or two torpedoes port side at frame 110. 0810 made preparations to get underway. Opened fire with 5" A.A. guns #2 and #4 on dive bombers. Ship commenced listing to port. 0815 U.S.S. OKLAHOMA capsized. 0820 ship was struck at frame 47 with torpedoes. 0825 opened fire with 5" A.A. battery at horizontal bombers. Ship shaken by four near bomb hits. 0830 bomb struck topside abreast casemate #1, frame 59, penetrated main deck and exploded on second deck, causing large fire. Ship listed 8 degrees to port, commenced counterflooding..."

These were the words chosen to succinctly record the most significant moments of *California's* career—the deck log entry for 7 December 1941. But, they fall short of telling the whole story, a story which includes four of *California's* men receiving the Medal of Honor.

Aggression by Germany and Japan had made it clear that the United States would soon be drawn into war. Hoping at least to prepare for this, or at best to avert war, the United States Fleet conducted Fleet Problem XXI in 1940. The war games were to be close enough to Japan to be noticed, but not so close as to be perceived as a threat. The Fleet's base of operations for this maneuver would be Hawaii. On 1 April 1940 the Battle Fleet, including flagship USS *California*, sailed from its time-honored home of San Pedro-Long Beach, bound for Hawaiian waters.

The exercise concluded, the Fleet was scheduled to sail for San Diego on 16 May 1940, but two days prior to sailing the Fleet was instead ordered to Lahaina Roads, the fleet's deep-water anchorage off Maui.

Following the successful use of aerial torpedoes by the British against the Italian fleet in Taranto in the Adriatic, it was decided that the Lahaina Roads anchorage was too vulnerable to that type of attack. The fleet instead would begin to anchor in Pearl Harbor, whose shallow depth it was believed made it invulnerable to aerial-launched torpedo attacks.

With that thought in mind, the fleet settled into a routine of one week of maneuvers followed by two weeks tied up in harbor, with Battle Fleet flagship *California's* usual spot being interrupted quay Fox Three (F-3), adjacent Ford Island.

It was at F-3 that *California* was moored on 7 December 1941, when the Japanese struck. While in the chaos of battle it was considered that the initial 0805 strike on the ship had been two torpedoes, subsequent examination of her hull showed that only a single torpedo struck at that time, followed by a second torpedo at 0820. Each struck below the armored belt, gouging holes 20

feet wide and 10 feet deep. Three waves of dive bombers also struck, two near misses causing relatively minor hull damage, and one hit igniting the fire noted in the deck log.

California was designed incorporating extensive anti-torpedo protection. In fact, both torpedos had breached the final interior void, and she should have been able to weather the hits. However, numerous manhole covers to the voids had been removed and others loosened. The Bureau of Ships 28 November 1942 War Damage Report lays much blame for the sinking of the *California* on these open voids, exacerbated further *"...because most of the watertight fittings on the third deck and below were open..."*

Captain Joel W. Bunkley, *California's* skipper, in his 26 January 1942 after action report stated that the ship was on the eve of a Material Condition inspection, requiring that the tanks and voids be vented; thus, according to his report, ten covers were removed. Five of these on the starboard side were closed by repair parties. However, salvage crews aboard *California* after her sinking found six covers open and twelve loosened on the port side—the side exposed to torpedo attack.

The 1946 report of the Joint Congressional Committee on the Investigation of the Pearl Harbor Attack, which numbered 15,000 pages, includes the notation that *"...the logs of the U.S.S. California, Maryland, Nevada and Tennessee have been examined for any record of inspections, and for any references concerning watertight integrity precedent to or in preparation for any inspections on 5, 6 or 7 December 1941, with negative results."*

How many or why manhole covers were removed will likely never been known with certainty, it is however virtually certain that had it not been for the swift action of Reserve Ensign Edgar M. Fain, who began counter flooding immediately, the flagship, like *Oklahoma* astern, would have capsized. *California*, initially under the command of senior line officer aboard Lt. Commander M. N. Little, was further hampered by the location of the initial torpedo hit. A fuel line was ruptured, allowing sea water to contaminate the fuel supply, and thus a power failure ensued at 0810. The lack of power prevented the operation of the antiaircraft ammunition hoists, and knocked out the ship's lighting.

The five-inch guns one and two had been designated ready guns, and had 50 rounds each in the ready ammunition. All other five-inch ammunition was stowed in the magazines below deck. Manpower was resorted to in order to pass ammunition, each shell weighing just over 50 pounds, up to the guns.

Into this human chain plunged a 250-kilogram (500-pound) bomb at 0845. Dropped from a Val, the bomb hit the upper deck adjacent to casemate one, at frame 59 on the starboard side, penetrating the upper and main decks before exploding against the armored second deck. This bomb caused many casualties, destroyed the watertight integrity of the first and second decks

between frames 26 and 100, and set fire to the midships.

One of the casualties of the bomb hit was Ensign Herbert C. Jones. Jones was supervising the passing of 5-inch ammunition between the second and third decks when the bomb hit, severely wounding him. Shipmates began evacuating Jones, but seeing that the compartment was in flames and that two of his rescuers themselves were wounded, ordered that he be left behind. Jones would be one of the four *California* crewmen awarded the Medal of Honor for their actions at Pearl Harbor—three of them, including Jones, posthumously.

Another casualty in the ammunition-passing brigade was Chief Radioman Thomas Reeves. Flooding had forced Reeves from the radio compartment, but he remained on the third deck, keeping the supply of ammunition moving, which is what he was doing when he was overcome my smoke and fire, perishing.

Reeves too was recognized with a Medal of Honor, as was Warrant Gunner Jackson Pharris. Suffering a concussion from the first torpedo hit, and twice losing consciousness, Pharris repeatedly entered flooding compartments to rescue men being submerged in water and oil, as well as passing ammunition. Pharris was *California's* only Medal of Honor recipient to survive 7 December.

Along with ammunition, compressed air was a requirement to operate *California's* antiaircraft guns. Machine's Mate First Class Robert Scott, whose battle station was the forward air compressor room, took his responsibility seriously. As the water rose in the compressor compartment, and forcing its evacuation, Scott told his shipmates *"This is my station and I will stay and give them air as long as the guns are going."* Scott drowned at his post, and was awarded the Medal of Honor, the citation reading *"For conspicuous devotion to duty, extraordinary courage, and complete disregard for his own life, above and beyond the call of duty."*

After the bomb hit, *California* was aflame aboard, and the waters of Pearl Harbor were aflame as well, the fuel oil leaking from *California* and her sisters blazing. Power had just been restored, and with it, pressure in the fire mains, when the bomb hit.

At 1002, Captain Bunkley, who had returned aboard at 0905, ordered *California* abandoned, due to the fires, especially the one drifting down upon her. At 1015 the winds had shifted, pushing the burning oil away from *California*, and the abandon ship order was rescinded.

But *California* and her crew could not overcome the circumstances—the open manholes, the loss of power and water pressure, the brief abandoning of ship, and the overall poor watertight integrity were too much. *California* was settling to the bottom of the harbor. It took three days, but settle she did, coming to rest in 16 feet of soft mud with a list of 5 ½-degrees port. Six officers and 92 men were killed or missing, and a further three officers and 58 men were wounded.

At 7:55 a.m. on 7 December, 1941, forces of the Imperial Japanese Navy attacked U.S. military installations on Oahu, the major focus being on the U.S. fleet at Pearl Harbor. In this Japanese photo of the early part of the attack, Battleship Row can be seen in its entirety. Closest to the camera is *Nevada*; while ahead of *Nevada* is *Arizona*, with repair ship *Vestal* moored outboard. Directly ahead of *Arizona* is *Tennessee*, with *West Virginia* moored outboard. Directly ahead of *Tennessee* is *Maryland*, moored outboard of *Maryland* is *Oklahoma*, who would capsize moment after this photo was taken. Ahead of *Maryland/Oklahoma* is fleet tanker *Neosho*—remarkably unscathed during the attack—she was later lost during the Battle of Coral Sea. Ahead of *Neosho*, and just barely in the photo, is *California*. (Naval History and Heritage Command)

Top left: Soon after the first wave of Japanese aircraft appeared over Pearl Harbor, Battleship Row was aflame with sinking and burning ships. In a photo taken on Ford Island facing northeast, the *California* has taken several torpedo hits and has started to list to port. (NARA) **Top right:** In a photo taken from the control tower on Ford Island, the *California* appears in the foreground, with little visible damage except the list to port. In the distance above *California*'s fantail is the hull of USS *Oklahoma*, which capsized minutes into the attack. (NARA) **Above left:** To prevent the listing *California* from capsizing, the crew acted to counterflood two boiler rooms and some hull blisters on the starboard side. These steps greatly reduced the list, but by the time this photo was taken around 1000, oil fires on the water were approaching. (NARA) **Above right:** At around 1000 hours, the burning oil was imperiling the ship, whose commanding officer, Capt. Joel Bunkley, gave the order to abandon ship. The crew temporarily abandoned ship at 1002 and began reboarding her after the flames cleared away at 1015. (Naval History and Heritage Command)

Top: The crew worked hard to keep *California* afloat as she gradually settled in the water. In this photo, the ship is still listing somewhat to port, and the main deck is nearly awash. In the left background, the column of smoke is from the burning destroyer *Shaw* (DD-373). **Above left:** The *California* is viewed from directly astern on 7 December, displaying a pronounced list. The national ensign is still waving defiantly from the staff on the stern. Straight ahead of the *California*, the USS *Shaw* continues to burn in Floating Dry Dock No. 2. (NARA) **Above right:** Smoke continues to envelope the *California* in the aftermath of the Japanese attack. Abeam the aft turrets and the forward turrets are the two moorings assigned to the *California*. Collectively, these massive concrete structures were designated Quay F-3. (NARA)

Top: Later on 7 December 1941, the *California* sits low in the water, with two small vessels standing by off her bow and a tugboat resting along her amidships. One of the ship's Vought Kingfisher scout planes is still on the catapult above turret number three. **Above:** In another photo in the aftermath of the attack, the *California* exhibits a light-colored area above where a torpedo hit below the armor belt abeam turret number two. Another torpedo hit abeam turret three, and a bomb penetrated several decks before exploding. (NARA, both)

Top left: Efforts continue to keep *California* afloat. In addition to the direct hits from the bomb and two torpedoes, a bomb struck the water near the port bow, causing a rupture below the waterline. A near miss of a bomb on the starboard side caused further damage. **Top right:** By the afternoon of 7 December, Navy vessels began to gather around *California* to provide pumping and firefighting support. The ship continued to sink, finally coming to rest firmly in the mud on the harbor bottom, at a list of approximately 5.5 degrees to port. **Above left:** In a photo dated 8 December 1941, a craft is alongside the port beam of *California* to render assistance; the superstructure is abeam the mainmast and the bow is to the right. Between the turrets are pumps and hoses, fighting a losing battle to dewater the hull. **Above right:** Several craft, including a minesweeper, lie alongside *California*. Even as the crew and other naval personnel struggled heroically to save the ship, gun crews in combat gear manned the antiaircraft battery in expectation of a Japanese follow-up attack. (NARA, all)

Salvage operations

Salvage operations aboard *California* began even before the sinking was complete, when the crew and yard personnel began removing the port secondary battery on 9 December, even as the ship was settling deeper into the harbor. *California* continued to sink until 11 December, at which time it was believed that she'd stopped settling into the mud. Work continued removing equipment and ammunition, but the she sank a further three inches between the 17th and 20th.

By that time an overall salvage plan was in place that would require sheet metal cofferdams—the material for which would not be delivered for 60 days. Should the settling rate continue, by that time the Prune Barge would be a further 5 feet in the Pearl Harbor mud. It was decided to remove the main battery, an estimated weight of 2,000 tons, in hopes of slowing the settling.

However, Commander James Rodgers, who was made project officer for the raising of *California*, after consulting with Pearl Harbor Public Works, did not believe that the sea bottom around *California* would support a cofferdam. Accordingly, Rodgers' plan was to make *California* watertight, and pump her out deck by deck. Patching *California*'s hull began on 25 January 1942. Instead of a steel cofferdam driven into the seabed, Rodgers had constructed wooden cofferdams attached to the quarterdeck and port forecastle, both underwater. On 25 February pumps began removing water at the rate of 20,000 gallons per minute, and as the water level began to slowly recede, divers began the grim task of removing *California*'s casualties.

In addition to the seawater, 200,000 gallons of fuel oil had floated throughout the ship, which had to be removed. *California* came afloat on 24 March 1942, and entered Drydock Number Two on 9 April. She would remain there until 7 June 1942, undergoing structural repairs. On 10 October she left Pearl Harbor under her own power, bound for Puget Sound.

Top right: The Navy mounted a massive salvage operation to bring as much of the fleet as possible back into action. Here, officers confer regarding salvage efforts for the *California*. At the center is Capt. Homer N. Wallin, salvage officer and Battle Fleet material officer. **Above left:** In preparation for salvaging the guns of turret three, in the foreground, the glacis and the roof of the gun house were removed. The guns of turret four, below and aft of turret three, would be salvaged later. (NARA) **Above right:** One of the 14-inch guns of turret three has been lifted clear of the gun house. An officer stands on protective slats where the forward cables are wrapped around the gun tube. To the lower right are another gun of the turret and the roof of turret number four.

Above left: The right 14-inch gun of turret number three is suspended above the turret, and two other 14-inch guns inside it remain to be removed. The sets of chains holding up the rear of the gun are fastened with clevises to brackets bolted to the gun breech. Below, workmen are standing in the open turret, whose roof and glacis had been removed to facilitate removal of the big guns. **Top right:** Several Navy craft including a small floating crane are assisting in efforts to prepare the *California* for recovery. To the far left, the 14- inch guns of turret one have been removed, and the guns of turret two, traversed to starboard, similarly have been salvaged. **Above right:** By now, the main deck of the *California* was resting below the surface, with the aircraft crane to the left indicating the location of the stern. The guns of turret three already had been salvaged, but the guns of turret four, traversed to starboard, await salvaging. (NARA, all)

USS CALIFORNIA 2/12/42
PREPARING TO LIFT MAIN MAST
FCP

2/13/42
F.C.P. U.S.S. CAL
MAINMAST

2/13/42
F.C.P. U.S.S. CA
MAINMAST,
CUT, AW

Above left: On 12 February 1942, preparations are underway to remove the mainmast from the *California*. For the task, a 150-ton floating crane was employed. This was part of the process of lightening the ship in advance of raising it and putting it in dry dock, and the antiquated cage mast already had been earmarked for replacement by a more modern mainmast. (NARA) **Top right:** A day after the preceding photo was taken, men with cutting torches had severed the many rods that made up the mainmast near the base, and the 150-ton floating crane was proceeding to remove it. The mast has begun to tilt but is secured by the crane. (Naval History and Heritage Command) **Above right:** In a close-up view taken around the same time as the preceding photo, on 13 February 1942, the mainmast of USS *California* has been cut by torches and is tilting aft, held steady by a floating crane. In the background is the rear of turret number three. (Naval History and Heritage Command)

U.S.S. CALIF.
3/10/42
PRELIMINARY
CLEANING #7

U.S.S. CALIF. 3/10/42

Top left: Before *California* could be dewatered, floated, and towed to dry dock, it was necessary to build cofferdams alongside the hull: on the port and starboard sides of the quarterdeck; at the stern (shown here on a barge on 27 February), and on the starboard forecastle. **Top right:** The forecastle cofferdam is in place on 27 February 1942, and pumps are discharging water from the hull. This cofferdam was built in eight sections, comprising vertical 4x12-inch planks with horizontal stiffeners, shored with heavy beams to the deck. The height of the sections varied from 26 to 31 feet high. The Pacific Bridge Co. constructed and installed the cofferdams for the *California*, and once these were in

place and the ship made watertight, the pumping of the hull began in earnest. **Above left:** As the water level finally began to subside within the *California*, work crews began the unpleasant task of cleaning the interior compartments and removing debris. These four men are taking a break during the preliminary cleaning of casemate seven on 10 March. **Above right:** The cofferdam along the port side of the forecastle is viewed on 10 March 1942. The upper part of the structure was shored with 6x8-inch wooden beams, and the top of the cofferdam was weighted-down with sandbags to counteract the structure's buoyancy. (NARA, all)

U.S.S. CALIF. 3/10/42
VIEW FORWARD

U.S.S. CALIF. 3/10/42
COFFERDAM BRACES
ON #3 TURRET

Above left: In a view of the foredeck from the starboard side of the navigating bridge on 10 March 1942, the top of the cofferdam and its shoring are visible in the distance. In the foreground is a gun tub, beyond which is turret number two, with a canvas cover thrown over it, and turret one. On the deck alongside turret two is a gypsy winch, and pump discharge pipes are in evidence. It would be several more days before the quarterdeck cofferdam was completed and dewatering could begin in earnest in that section of the ship.
Top right: The progress of construction of the quarterdeck cofferdam is documented in a

10 March 1942 photograph facing aft from the starboard side of the navigating bridge. In the foreground is the starboard boat derrick. Some shoring was braced against the turrets. **Above right:** In another 10 March view, the section of starboard quarterdeck cofferdam in the foreground is heavily braced with wooden shores against the barbette of turret number three. On the opposite side of the turret, the port quarterdeck cofferdam is visible. (NARA, all)

Text on photo: U.S.S. Calif. 3/18/42 Sleeping quarters Main deck port by #1 turret looki aft.

Top: The quarterdeck cofferdam is viewed from off *California's* port stern on 19 March 1942. A large hose amidships is discharging a copious amount of water. Inside the quarterdeck cofferdam, water still covered the port side of the deck nearly to the center-line hatches. **Above left:** On 7 December 1941 a 250-kilogram bomb pierced the starboard upper deck at about frame 59 and crashed through the main deck, exploding on the second deck. Shown here in an 18 March 1942 photo is some of the damage from the explosion on the main deck. **Above right:** In another 18 March photo, an oily muck coats every surface in the sleeping quarters to the port side of turret number one on the main deck. Cleaning the interior of the ship was a tedious, disagreeable, and dangerous job undertaken by hundreds of workers. (NARA, all)

U.S.S. Calif 3-22-42
Admirals Cabin

U.S.S. Calif. 3/21/42
Cofferdam Fantail

Above left: On 22 March 1942, debris, overturned furniture, and standing water were encountered in the admiral's cabin. As the ship was gradually dewatered and salvage crews made their way from compartment to compartment, they removed thousands of items, from ammunition, spoiled food, furnishings, and documents to mechanical and electrical equipment, for repair, refurbishing, or disposal. By the end of this work day, crews had collected 208,000 gallons of loose oil from within the *California*. **Top right:** The extent of

the intricate shoring of the quarterdeck cofferdam is apparent in this 21 March 1942 photo. By now, the main deck was clear of water, and the water level had subsided to just below the second deck at the longitudinal centerline of the ship. (NARA) **Above right:** On 22 March 1942, the forward part of *California* is observed from the port side. Although the ship still sat low in the water, efforts to dewater the hull were succeeding, and the buoyancy of the quarterdeck cofferdam had caused the stern to rise two feet. (NARA)

Top left: The *California* is viewed from 20 degrees off the port bow on 25 March 1942. The upper part of turret one and the three ports in the glacis for the 14-inch guns are just visible above the cofferdam. A pump discharge pipe is spewing water over the bow. **Above left:** On 30 March 1942, USS *California* is observed from the starboard side. The stern section of the cofferdam straddled the fantail of the ship directly forward of the aircraft-handling crane. The cofferdam was built around turret four's gun barrels, pointing to starboard. **Above right:** The *California* is viewed from the front on 30 March 1942, showing the current location of the waterline and also the forward end of the forecastle cofferdam. Sandbags are piled up several yards aft of the bow. Several men are standing by the hawse pipes, inspecting the anchor chains; the preceding day, preparations had been made for removing the anchors, one of the steps taken to lighten the ship. (NARA, all)

Above left: The *California* is viewed from a higher angle from off the bow on 30 March. To the rear of the sandbags across the forecastle is a Pomona deep-well pump, with a horizontal discharge pipe running forward to above the bow. The shoring beams of the forecastle cofferdam are in view. More pump-discharge pipes are visible in on the starboard side of the forecastle and in the background. **Top right:** As seen from off the port stern on 4 April, the stern now is well above water. The maximum waterline that had existed high up on the cofferdam is clearly visible. The ship had been floated free of the mud on 24 March but had required further dewatering. **Above right:** The *California* is viewed off her starboard bow on 4 April after being floated. On this date the ship had a draft of approximately 41 feet. The forecastle cofferdam had been removed over the past day, and soon the ship would go into dry dock for further repairs. (NARA, all)

USS CALIFORNIA ENROUTE TO
NO. 2 DRYDOCK
4/9/42

USS Calif. 4-9-42
Torpedo Hit Amidship
Port Side

Top left: Onboard pumps still spewing water over the side, USS *California* has been re-floated, the holes in the hull have been patched, the caissons have been removed, and the ship is being towed by tugboats to Dry Dock No. 2, Pearl Harbor, on 9 April 1942. **Top right:** *California* enters Dry Dock No. 2 on 9 April. In order to reduce her draft sufficiently to allow her to cross the sill at the entrance to the dry dock, as much weight as possible had been removed from her, including the conning tower, removed a few days earlier. **Above left:** Divers had been able to view and assess the underwater damage to the *California* before she was refloated, but once the ship was dry-docked, the full extent of the damage became more apparent. Here is the area where a torpedo struck amidships. (NARA) **Above right:** The damage from the after torpedo hit is shown in a 9 April 1942 photo. The inner bulkhead is visible through the breach. That the *California* was floated and moved to dry dock without the necessity of patches was testimony to the ship's excellent design. (NARA, all)

USS *California* is positioned in Dry Dock No. 2, and most of the water has been pumped out of the dock, allowing repair crews to observe the full extent of the damage incurred on December 7. Below the waterline in the foreground is where the hull suffered damage from a near miss of a bomb and, subsequently, from a vapor explosion during the salvage operation. (NARA)

USS Calif 4-9-42 Damage by near miss from bomb port bow

Above left: In a view of the bow of the *California* in Dry Dock No. 2, visible between frames 11 and 15 on the port side is damage caused both by the explosion of a Japanese bomb that narrowly missed the ship and by an explosion inside the bow on 5 April 1942. The latter explosion blew off a patch that had been installed over the original breach in the hull. Rather than re-patch the hole, it was left open for the short tow to Dry Dock No. 2 four days later. **Top right:** The damage to the port side of the hull from a near-miss of a Japanese bomb on 7 December, compounded by an internal explosion on 5 April, is observed from the side on 9 April 1942. The latter explosion occurred inside compartment A-201-A. **Above right:** The scale of the hole in the port side of the hull from the near-miss of a bomb is made more impressive by the presence of a work crew inside the opening in a 10 April 1942 photograph. The force of the bomb explosion pushed several plates of the shell inward. (NARA, all)

The *California* is seen from the rear in dry dock on 10 April 1942. The mud line is faintly visible along the lower part of the hull, extending to the upper part of the rudder. The ship's settling into the mud had not caused significant damage to rudder or propellers. (NARA)

Top left: The starboard side of *California* is observed from the bow aft in dry dock. The original caption of the photo indicated that it illustrated the location of the mud line where the ship had settled after the 7 December attack; it is the faint, wavy line toward the bottom. **Above left:** Another 10 April 1942 photograph shows the underside of the hull below where the after torpedo struck. In the background are the two port propellers and propeller shafts. The port docking keel of the ship is resting on keel blocks, which supported the ship. **Above right:** The hole where the after torpedo penetrated on 7 December is observed at an angle from aft. The torpedo strike created an opening between frames 99 and 104 and extended down from the belt armor. After penetrating the shell, the torpedo penetrated longitudinal bulkhead number one, buckled bulkhead two severely and caused two fragment holes in it, buckled bulkheads three and four but did not penetrate them, and caused no damage to the innermost bulkhead, number five, except causing a slight bulge in it. (NARA, all)

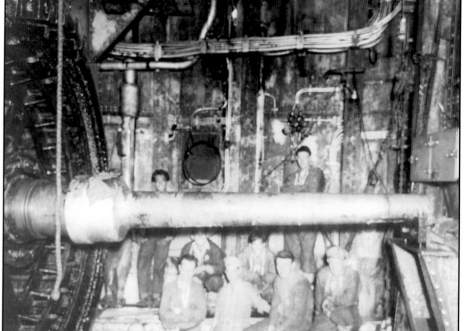

Above left: Most of the wreckage in the bomb-damaged area on the starboard side of the *California* between frames 46 and 56 had been removed by the time this photo was taken on 21 April 1942. The view is on the outside of the hull looking aft. The blast from a near-miss bomb had dished-in the side of the hull in this area, with a maximum inward deflection of approximately 14 inches at frame 52. Aside from some deflection to longitudinal bulkhead number one, interior damage was limited. **Top right:** Damage caused by the one bomb that was a direct hit on the *California* during the 7 December attack is viewed on the main deck looking forward on 13 April. The closest stanchion at the center of the photo was at frame 61 on the starboard side of the ship. **Above right:** The four electric motors that propelled the ship were underwater for months, and during salvage operations there was concern that they would be irreparable. However, all four motors were rehabilitated. Here, workers pose by an extension shaft supporting a rotor. (NARA, all)

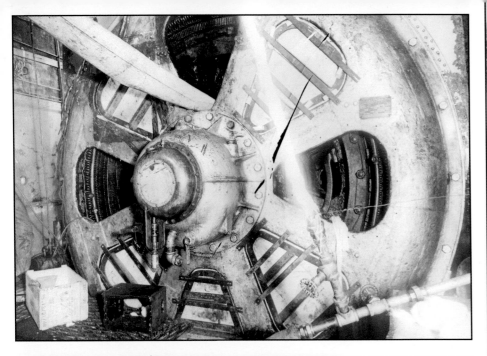

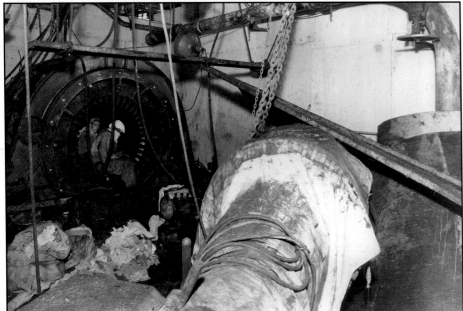

Top left: In a photo taken on the same date as the preceding one, 17 April 1942, a method of sealing holes in the end shield of motor number four is illustrated. Two of the main motors were repaired at Pearl Harbor and two were repaired later at Puget Sound. **Above left:** Temporary plywood bulkheads have been installed around the forward turbogenerator room in a 20 May 1942 photo. General Electric and the Pearl Harbor Navy Yard shared the task of rehabilitating the electrical systems: reportedly the largest such field job to date. **Above right:** Forward propulsion generator number one is viewed from the collector-ring end. Before the USS *California* could depart for further repairs and modernization at Bremerton under her own propulsion, it was necessary to rewind two of her generators. There were two main propulsion generators, located on the centerline below decks, each rated at 15,000 kilovolt-amperes, and these provided electrical power for the four propulsion motors. (NARA, all)

OFFICIAL PHOTOGRAPH
NOT TO BE RELEASED
FOR PUBLICATION
NAVY YARD PEARL HARBOR T.H.

Top left: As part of the rehabilitation of the *California*'s propulsion generators, field coils are being baked in an oven in a plywood enclosure inside one of the buildings at the Pearl Harbor Navy Yard on 6 May 1942. To the far left are coils on a varnishing rack. **Top right:** During the rehabilitation of one of the *California*'s propulsion generators, workers are starting the first coil on the number-one rotor. The man to the left is seating the coil using a mallet. More coils to be installed are at the ready on a rack above the rotor. **Above left:** On 6 June 1942, with only one day left to go before USS *California* departs from dry dock at Pearl Harbor, a worker on a scaffold performs final touches to the area between frames 93 and 108 on the port side of the hull where a torpedo struck on 7 December. **Above right:** Another 6 June 1942 photograph documents where repairs were made to the hull where one of the Japanese torpedoes hit, between frames 6 and 21 on the port side. The inclined angle of the strakes, or tiers of shell plates, in this area of the ship is emphasized. (NARA, all)

Top left: The repairs to the hull of USS *California* on the starboard side between frames 49 and 57 are shown in this 6 June 1942 photograph. Running along the top of the photo is the belt armor, and to the lower right is the rear end of one of the ship's bilge keels. **Top right:** Repairs to her hull completed, the *California* departed from Dry Dock No. 2 at Pearl Harbor on 7 June 1942. Here, the dry dock is being pumped full of water in order to float the ship. The water level is still several yards below the bottom of the boot topping. **Above left:** Within moments of when the preceding photo was taken, this one was snapped from the top of the dry dock. Most of the hull had been repainted in dry dock, but the bow exhibited a mix of new gray paint, old paint, and a patchy dark-colored coating. **Above right:** The *California* is moments away from floating as the water level rises in the dry dock at Pearl Harbor on 7 June 1942. The 14-inch guns of turret four, which had not been removed, are now trained aft. Temporary ducts are in evidence at various places. (NARA, all)

Top left: *California* is observed from directly astern just before undocking. Until this date, Hawaii and Pearl Harbor had been under threat of a new Japanese advance, but that advance was stopped dead in its tracks and repulsed by the Pacific Fleet at the Battle of Midway. **Top right:** The ship is viewed from off the port stern just before undocking on 7 June 1942. The aircraft-handling crane still stands tall on the fantail. The gaping front of turret three is in view. Gone is the mainmast, but the cage-type foremast survives—for the time being. **Above left:** *California* has departed Dry Dock No. 2 on 7 June 1942 following a two-month sojourn in that facility. Following undocking, the ship was moved to another dock at Pearl Harbor for more months of outfitting before proceeding to Bremerton for modernization. **Above right:** The recently refurbished and remounted 14-inch guns of turrets one and two are viewed. In the background is a massive floating crane, which had been employed in remounting the guns. The crane was kept busy around the harbor performing repairs and salvage. (NARA, all)

After leaving dry dock, the *California* remained in dock at Pearl Harbor Navy Yard for further work until October 1942. In an aerial view on 18 July 1942, a large floating crane is alongside her starboard bow, placing a gun in turret one. (Official U.S. Navy Photograph, from the collections of the Naval History and Heritage Command.)

Top left: *California* is shown while docked at Pearl Harbor for additional refitting and repair work. In a view from the bridge, all 14-inch guns of turrets one and two, not present in the preceding photo, are remounted. Barrels in the water indicate torpedo nets. **Top right:** In a view forward from the fantail of *California* on 9 August 1942, the guns of turret three have been remounted. The ship had a greatly altered skyline by this time; after leaving dry dock in June, the cage-type foremast had been removed. **Above left:** Since leaving dry dock, the *California* had received further painting, as seen here from off the port stern on 9 August 1942. The hull and superstructure were now a dark color, with the battleship's number, 44, painted on the stern; the after turrets were lighter. **Above right:** In another 9 August 1942 photo, the forward turrets and the superstructure are viewed from the fore-castle. The ship now had a spare appearance, having lost its conning tower, masts, and certain other structures and equipment during salvage and repair operations. (NARA, all)

Top left: A 7 October 1942 photo documents the generator and distribution switchboard in the after turbogenerator room after the equipment had been reconditioned. Restoring such sophisticated electrical equipment to functionality had been a monumental task. (NARA) **Top right:** One of the 400-kilowatt ship's service turbogenerators (SSTGs) in the after turbogenerator room is shown in operation on 14 September 1942.

Each of the two turbogenerator rooms had three SSTGs for providing electricity to ancillary systems. (NARA) **Above:** At 1255 on 10 October 1942, USS *California* departed from Berth B-22 at Pearl Harbor en route to Bremerton, Washington, with Convoy 4217. Here, the ship is proceeding past Ford Island, with the southern end of the Wai'anae Range in the distance. (A.D. Baker III collection)

Return to Puget Sound

That *California* was able to return to Puget Sound was in no small part due to the efforts of Hyman Rickover. Rickover, who would gain fame as the Father of the Nuclear Navy, was at the time head of the Electrical Section of the Bureau of Ships. Counter to earlier thoughts that *California's* electrical drive system had been destroyed by 105 days of submersion, Rickover demand that one alternator and two motors be rebuilt in place at Pearl. Aided by GE, this was accomplished, and *California* made the 9-day crossing to the mainland unassisted.

At 1524 on Monday 19 October 1942 *California* moored at berth 6-B of Puget Sound Navy Yard. *California* would remain tied up at Puget Sound until 23 May 1943, when she was moved into drydock. At 1850 she settled onto keel blocks in what would be her home until December of that year. During this time *California* would undergo the most significant transformation of her career.

Her superstructure was removed to the second deck. Replacing the cage masts and twin funnels would be a single funnel, and a modern conning tower. Although the new conning tower resembled that of the *South Dakota* class battleships, it was actually taken over from a cruiser design. Adding to the *South Dakota* resemblance was the installation of eight 5-inch/38 twin mounts. These dual-purpose weapons would not only be effective against surface targets, but also give considerable weight to *California's* antiaircraft defenses. Providing additional protection from further aerial aggression was a battery of 56 40mm guns in 14 quad mounts and 72 20mm automatic cannons. All of these repairs and modifications were brought about through 865,835 man-days of labor.

California moved to an anchorage in Puget Sound on 16 January 1944, and after three days of provisioning, made a trial run. On 31 January she sailed for Long Beach for a shakedown and training period, and on 5 May, along with fellow Pearl Harbor veteran *Maryland* and other battleships, left San Francisco, bound again for Pearl Harbor.

Top right: An overhead view taken off the port bow of the *California* at Navy Yard Puget Sound on 10 January 1944 includes a good view of the big "bedspring" antenna of the SK air-search radar on the foremast. Atop the foremast and the mainmast are SG surface-search radars. **Above left:** The port amidships area of USS *California* is observed from above in another 10 January 1944 image. Measure 32, Design 16D camouflage has been painted on the ship. Some of the gun mounts and fire-control stations installed in the modernization are in view. **Above right:** On the same date as the preceding photo, a cameraman took this image to document the radar installations on the *California* from the port quarter. The SK radar antenna towers above the smokestack. To the right are the main-battery and secondary-battery directors. (NARA, all)

Above left: The mainmast is viewed from an elevated perspective to the port side on 10 January 1944. At the top is the SK radar antenna. Below and to the front of the radar work platform is the forward main-battery control station, with a Mk. 34 director with a Mk. 8 radar antenna on top. **Above right:** In a 10 January 1944 view from amidships, at the center is the port Mk. 37 director and Mk. 4 radar antenna. The four Mk. 37 directors installed on the ship during the 1942-1944 modernization were part of the fire-control system for the secondary battery of 5-inch/38-caliber gun mounts. (NARA, both)

Above left: The mainmast of USS *California* is observed from an elevated position on the port beam on 10 January 1944. At the top of the mainmast are a work platform with railing and the aft SG surface-search radar antenna. The mainmast is mounted with braces to the aft main fire-control station. **Above right:** The starboard Mk. 37 director and Mk. 4 radar antenna are viewed facing aft. The four Mk. 37 directors and Mk. 4 radars were part of a complex fire-control system, linked to a fire-control computer, a rangekeeper, and a stable element. The directors were in effect the eyes of this system. (NARA, both)

Above left: The starboard Mk. 37 director with the Mk. 4 antenna on top is viewed from the front. The Mk. 4 radar was used to acquire and designate targets; for example it could detect a destroyer at 16,000 yards. The Mk. 37 director contained an optical rangefinder and several operators. **Above right:** The front of the forward, or Number 1, Mk. 37 director with a Mk. 4 antenna is observed. Sighting hatches were provided for the crew, who trained (traversed), pointed (adjusted the elevation), cross-leveled, and otherwise controlled the rangefinder and radar. Projecting from the sides of the director was the rangefinder. (NARA, both)

Top: In a view from the foremast, directly below is the forward Mk. 37 director for the secondary battery, with a Mk. 4 radar antenna mounted on top. Below and to the front of the director, on top of the conning tower, is a quad 40mm gun mount and tub. **Below left:** In this view of the top of the foremast, at the top is the antenna of the aft SG microwave surface-search set. Below it is a service platform with hoop-shaped safety rails. Jutting from the platform are a BK "ski pole" transponder antenna and an OAA-2 radar antenna. (NARA, both) **Below:** As part of *California*'s rebuild, eight 5-inch, 38-caliber dual purpose mounts were installed. Along with the mounts came Mark 37 gun directors and analog computers that were used to bring the guns to bear.

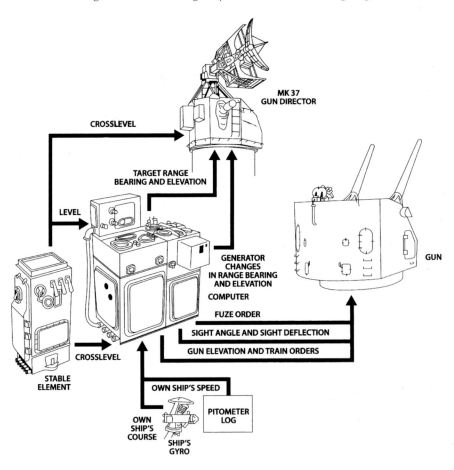

MK 37
GUN DIRECTOR

CROSSLEVEL

TARGET RANGE
BEARING AND ELEVATION

LEVEL

GUN

GENERATOR
CHANGES
IN RANGE BEARING
AND ELEVATION

COMPUTER

FUZE ORDER

SIGHT ANGLE AND SIGHT DEFLECTION

CROSSLEVEL

GUN ELEVATION AND TRAIN ORDERS

STABLE
ELEMENT

OWN SHIP'S SPEED

OWN
SHIP'S
COURSE

SHIP'S
GYRO

PITOMETER
LOG

On 17 January 1944, USS *California* departed from Pier 3B at Navy Yard Puget Sound and dropped anchor at Anchorage C, Sinclair Inlet, Bremerton, Washington. The following series of photos of the ship was taken at that anchorage the following day. (A.D. Baker III collection)

Top: The *California*'s new camouflage scheme, Measure 32, Design 16B, is seen to good effect from this angle. Mounted in tandem on the catapult on the fantail are two Vought OS2U Kingfisher scout planes painted in three-color camouflage schemes. **Above:** USS *California* is viewed from the aft starboard quarter at Anchorage C on 18 January 1944. During her 1942-1944 modernization, anti-torpedo blisters had been added to the sides of the hull, increasing the beam from 97.3 feet as built to 114 feet. (A.D. Baker III collection, both)

Top left: The USS *California* is seen from directly aft off Bremerton on 18 January 1944. On either side of the stern were recent additions: two gun tubs for a single 20mm antiaircraft mount, with tapering fairings extending downward along the sides of the hull. **Top right:** USS *California* is viewed from off the bow while anchored at Sinclair Inlet off Bremerton, Washington, on 18 January 1944, showing the interface of the port and starboard sides of the Measure 32, Design 16D, at the stem. **Above:** The entire scope of the Measure 32, Design 16D camouflage scheme on the port side of the *California* is displayed. Vertical surfaces were painted in Dull Black (BK), Ocean Gray (5-O), and Light Gray (5-L), and horizontal surfaces in Ocean Gray and Deck Blue (20-B). (NARA, all)

After undergoing degaussing, a process to reduce the ship's magnetic signature, on 24 January 1944, the *California* proceeded along Puget Sound to Port Angeles, Washington, as shown in this photo. Next, the ship would continue to undergo trials for several more days. (A.D. Baker III collection)

Top: During the run to Port Angeles on 25 January 1944, the ship was photographed in the Straits of Juan de Fuca at 1420 at a speed of 8 knots and a true bearing of 270 degrees. During this day's cruise, the crew performed various drills, including gunnery. (A.D. Baker III collection) **Above:** Within moments of the preceding photograph, a Navy photographer in an aircraft snapped this view of the *California* steaming in the Straits of Juan de Fuca. The two Vought OS2U Kingfishers that had been on the catapult a week earlier had been removed. (NARA)

Above left: The *California* is viewed off her stern while proceeding to Port Washington at 1420 on the afternoon of 25 January 1944. The guns of turret four, previously elevated, now have been lowered. The new 20mm gun galleries on the deck and on turret three are visible. **Above right:** The same aerial photographer who took the preceding views of the *California* in the Straits of Juan de Fuca on 25 January 1944 snapped this view of the ship from off the bow. Six days later, the *California* would depart from Washington on a shakedown cruise. (NARA, both)

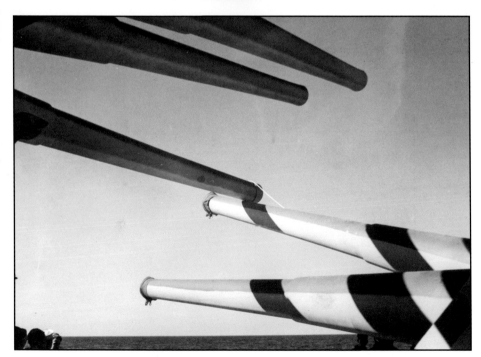

Top left: Atop the mainmast is the aft SG surface-search radar antenna. The SG was the first USN surface-search radar, developed in 1940 and first tested at sea in June 1941. In addition to being able to detect ships and low-flying aircraft, it also was useful in navigation. **Top right:** During the *California's* shakedown off her namesake state's coast in March 1944, a major gaffe occurred when several of the 14-inch/50-caliber guns of turrets three and four collided during gunnery drill, resulting in the jamming-together of two of the guns. **Above left:** The jammed 14-inch/50-caliber guns of turrets three and

four are viewed from another angle. The guns involved were the left tube of turret three and the center one of turret four. A line has been rigged near the muzzle of the turret-three gun to free it. **Above right:** In a view taken from atop turret four, sailors have fashioned a rig to free the 14-inch gun barrels, involving a line from the turret-three gun to a compound block-and-tackle rig, with steel cables running from the double sheaves to winches on the deck below. (NARA, all)

USS California (BB44) 1944

When *California* left Puget Sound at the completion of her post-Pearl Harbor rebuild, her superstructure had been completely replaced. Replacing the earlier dual cage masts and two funnels were a cruiser conning tower and single funnel, which along with the 5-inch twin mounts gave the old battlewagon a distinctly modern appearance.

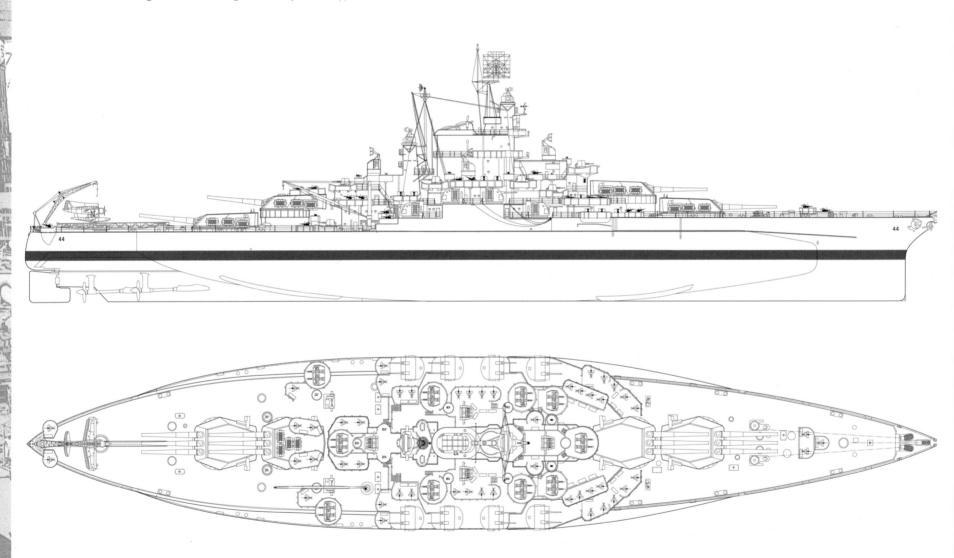

California was painted in camouflage Measure 32-16d. The irregular pattern was intended to make it difficult for observers to determine the distance, course and speed of the vessel.

Top: USS *California* performed frequent shore-bombardment missions during U.S. Navy operations in the Marianas in the summer of 1944. Here, in a photograph taken from USS *New Mexico*, the battleship is shelling Guam during the invasion of that island in July. (NARA)

Above: A little over 30 months after being put out of the war at Pearl Harbor, U.S.S. *California* reentered the fray, participating in the shelling of Saipan starting on D-1, 14 June 1944. This photo is thought to show the pre-invasion shelling as seen from the *California*. (NARA)

Top left: While *California's* batteries were firing on Saipan at 0910 on 14 June, a Japanese howitzer round struck the forward starboard corner of the main-battery fire-control platform on the 09 deck, penetrating three decks, killing one man and wounding several. **Top right:** The location where the Japanese shell penetrated the 09 deck is viewed from another angle. The shell rendered the exterior-communication facilities in the pilothouse out of action, and severed cables started an electrical fire over the chart desk in that compartment. **Above left:** This view was taken from 09 deck looking down at the shell penetrations through the 08 and 07 decks. The official report of the battle damage estimated that the projectile was a howitzer shell of from 4 inches to 5 inches in diameter, fired from a range of about 5,000 yards. **Above right:** While *California's* quad 40mm gun mount number five was firing at an approaching Japanese plane off Saipan on 18 June 1944, rounds from that mount struck both barrels of 5-inch gun mount number three, necessitating the replacement of both 5-inch gun barrels. (NARA, all)

Collision with USS *Tennessee* (BB-43)

After having bombarded Tinian from 23 July to 31 July 1944, *California* steamed to Guam, providing gunfire support from 2 August until 8 August, before anchoring at Eniwetok on 9 August. Three days later, *California* joined *Tennessee* and *Pennsylvania*, as well as eight cruisers and destroyers to form Task Unit 53.5.4 and steamed for the New Hebrides, pausing on 21 August for a Crossing the Line ceremony presided over by King Neptune.

The revelry gave way to tragedy just before dawn on 23 August. While steaming at 16 knots, at 0435 *Tennessee* was observed turning erratically. At 0441½ a transmission was received from Commander, Battleship Division Two, to disregard the movements of the *Tennessee*. *California*'s commanding officer, Captain Burnett, heard this transmission in his sea cabin, and immediately went through the connecting door to the pilot house. At 0444 *California*'s Combat Information Center (CIC) reported *Tennessee* on base course and 1,200 yards distant. At this time *Tennessee* was seen broad on the port bow, and appeared well clear, so at 0445 Capt. Burnett returned to his cabin. At 0448½ the Commander Battleship Division Two radioed "Steering casualty on Imperial"—indicating *Tennessee* had lost steering control. Immediately, the CIC announced that *Tennessee* had closed within 800 yards and could no longer be tracked by radar. Less than five seconds after the warning from BatDiv2, *California*'s rudder was put full right and the starboard engine ordered to back at full speed. This maneuver, known as twisting the ship, is the most forceful way to turn a warship. *California* went to Collision Quarters and both battleships turned on their running lights. At 0449½ *Tennessee* struck *California* on the port bow at about frame 21. The sound of rending steel shattered the night as the two ships met and swung to parallel courses, coming into contact over about two-thirds of their lengths, before finally the reaction to the impact pushed them apart.

California's shell was opened to the sea from frames 16 to 35. The forecastle deck was forced upward three feet for the same distance. Five-inch mount 8 was out of commission, the foundation damaged, training unit broken and roller path displaced. *California*'s men suffered even more—eight men were killed or went over the side from berthing compartment A608L. *Tennessee*'s bow had pierced the sick bay and berthing compartments for the 2nd and 5th Divisions. Fortunately, 2nd Division was standing watch, or casualties would have been even higher. Two men were alive but trapped in the area, requiring 7/8-inch steel plating to be cut away to free them. Seven more men were injured. By 0750 the rescue of the trapped personnel had been completed, and the bow, which had been down 22 inches due to flooding shortly after the collision, had been trimmed via counter flooding to being only down 5 inches. *California* resumed steaming at 16 knots, shoring bulkheads and stretching canvas in an effort to minimize water intrusion. Most of the flooding was unfortunately in the sick bay area.

California arrived in Pallikulo Bat about 0730 on 24 August 1944, and lay to behind an antitorpedo net, her anchors inoperable due to flooding of the anchor windlass motor control. As the sun began to set floating drydock ABSD-1 reported that it was ready to receive *California*, and in darkness and unfavorable seas the battleship was eased into the drydock at 2030, and by 2105 she was resting on keel blocks. A survey of the damage discovered, in addition to the damage to mount 8, 104 crew bunks and 60 lockers were destroyed, along with all the photographic darkroom equipment, all the canvas stores, about half of the freshwater system and the degaussing equipment heavily damaged.

It would take the crew of ABSD-1, along with the repair ship USS *Briareus* (AR-12) and *California*'s own men 18 days to repair the ship, with *California* leaving the drydock on 11 September 1944.

Left: While cruising toward Espiritu Santo in the early hours of 23 August 1944, USS *Tennessee* suffered a steering failure, colliding with her sister ship USS *California*. This photo, taken on the *California*, is the first of a series documenting the damages. In the collision, *Tennessee*'s stem crashed into the port bow of *California*, causing considerable damage to the side of the hull and to the forward decks. The force of the crash caused the forecastle, or upper, deck to buckle three feet upward between frames 16 and 35 and ruptured the main deck, one level below the forecastle deck, leaving it open to the elements from frame 16 to frame 35. (NARA)

Top left: The forecastle deck is observed from a different perspective, showing the tarpaulins covering the buckled deck. Several lower decks were ruptured as well, and various spaces in the forward part of the hull were flooded, necessitating shoring and dewatering. **Top right:** Taken around the same time as the preceding photos, this view was shot from the roof of turret one looking down at the forecastle deck. The force of the collision had shoved the edge of the deck up three feet, sloping inboard for a distance of 20 feet. **Above:** On the day following the collision with the *Tennessee*, the *California* is anchored in Pallikulo Bat, Espiritu Santo, where the damage was surveyed. The huge rent in the port side of the hull and the three-foot-high buckling of the forecastle deck are in view. (NARA, all)

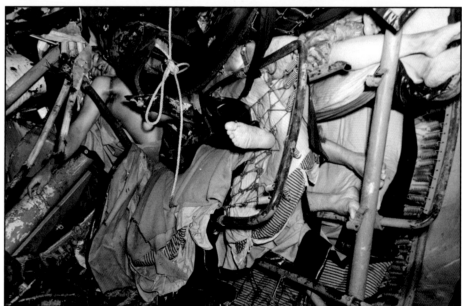

Top: The rent in the hull is observed from a closer perspective. Inside, officers and men are inspecting the devastation. In addition to this huge opening, there were numerous indentations in the shell of the hull, up to 14 inches wide and 5 inches deep. **Above left:** After the collision of 23 August 1944, the *California* set course for the U.S. Navy base at Espiritu Santo, where there was a floating dry dock that could accommodate the battleship for repairs. This image through the void in the hull was taken during that run. **Above right:** After the collision, it was determined that one crewman was killed, six were missing, and eight were injured, but subsequently five of the missing were found dead in their bunks in berthing compartment A-608-L, as seen here, and their remains were recovered. (NARA, all)

Top left: Some of the wreckage inside the hull of the *California* is shown. Among a long list of damaged and destroyed structures and fixtures, 17 CPOs' bunks, 14 CPOs' lockers, 104 crew bunks, and 60 crew lockers were destroyed as a result of the 23 August collision. **Above left:** Personnel survey the damage in the hull of the *California* after the ship arrived in port at Espiritu Santo the day after the collision. The main living spaces that were ruptured were the sick bay, the CPOs' bunkroom, and the 2nd and 5th Division compartments. **Right:** Personnel watch as the man with the cutting tool tries to cut through some steel. The "25 # SHIP'S SIDE" and "MAIN DECK / FR. 20" signs appear to have been applied as an identification guide to help repair crews detect the locations of specific frame numbers in the confused mass of twisted metal. (NARA, all)

Above left: The large rent in the hull is viewed from farther away. Several of the degaussing coils, which acted to reduce the magnetic signature of the ship, were destroyed. Other materials destroyed included but by no means were limited to 7,000 feet of electrical cables; 40 overhead lighting fixtures; 17 electric fans. **Top right:** The collision totally destroyed the structural framing of the hull in a significant area of the port side, as can be seen in this view taken from abeam the ship, looking into the rent in the hull. A sailor below the "25 # SHIP'S SIDE" sign is wielding a power cutting tool. (NARA) **Above right:** During the 23 August collision, the stem of the *Tennessee* caused a series of indentations to the port side of the hull of the *California* aft of the large rupture toward the bow. At the center of this photo is a large dent in the hull below the forward port 5-inch gun mount. (NARA, all)

Top left: The collision did considerable damage to 5-inch/38-caliber mount number eight (the rearmost of the four mounts on the port side), wracking and denting the gun shield and damaging or destroying a long list of internal components of the gun mount. (NARA)

Top right: Although it is not particularly noticeable in this photo, the collision pushed the gun shield, or gun house, of 5-inch mount number eight to the left and caused a large dent in the right side of the shield, forcing the gun ports out of alignment with the gun tubes. (NARA) **Above left:** Inside California's 5-inch/38-caliber mount number eight, the 23

August 1944 collision with the *Tennessee* caused a considerable inventory of damages, such as these floor plates and platforms over the hydraulic training unit, which have been knocked loose. (NARA) **Above right:** On the night of 24 August 1944, one day after the collision, USS California entered floating dry dock USS ABSD-1 at Pallikulo Bat, Espiritu Santo, for repairs. The ship is shown in the dry dock on that night, with scores of flood-lights turned on to illuminate her. (USS Tennessee Museum)

Top left: By the time this nighttime photo was taken in the floating dry dock, much of the damaged areas toward the bow *California* had been cut away in preparation for reconstruction. The tapered structure inside the hull with the hole cut in it is the port anchor-chain pipe. **Top right:** In a view from a slightly different perspective than the preceding one and taken during daylight, the area to be reconstructed is shown. Numerous oxy-acetylene bottles for cutting and welding are on the forecastle deck. Reconstruction of the framing will follow. **Above left:** The extent to which the force of the collision of the *California* and the *Tennessee* caused the forecastle deck to buckle as much as three feet upward is particularly apparent in this view taken in floating dry dock USS ABSD-I at Pallikulo Bat, Espiritu Santo. **Above right:** Navy work crews labor with cutting torches to cut away damaged materials inside the hull of USS *California* in floating dry dock. Once that material has been removed, the rebuilding of the structures damaged in the collision will commence. (NARA, all)

Top left: From the time the preceding photo and this photo were taken, considerable progress had been made on repairs. The bulge in the forecastle deck was being corrected and new deck beams installed. Below the forecastle deck, the main deck had been rebuilt. (USS Tennessee Museum) **Above left:** Plating is being installed on the hull of USS *California* in early September 1944. It is a tribute to the advanced-base repair crews of the

Navy that such complicated repairs could be performed on a battleship in such a brief timeframe, far from Stateside shipyards. (USS Tennessee Museum) **Above right:** *California* is viewed from astern on 8 September. On the fantail, the patterns of the lighter Ocean Gray paint (5-0) contrast with the darker Deck Blue paint (20-B). The light-colored object in front of the aircraft crane is a screen of some type. (A.D. Baker III collection)

On 11 September 1944, the *California* is being refloated. In 19 days, navy crews at Espiritu Santo had repaired the catastrophic damages the ship suffered in the collision with the *Tennessee*, and BB-44 was ready to resume active operations. (A.D. Baker III collection)

Top left: At 1210 on the afternoon of 11 September 1944, the *California*, now fully water-borne, began backing out of dry dock USS ABSD-1. This aerial photo was taken a few minutes later as a tugboat on the starboard side of the stern assists in steering the ship. (A.D. Baker III collection) **Top right:** Moments after the preceding photo was taken, another tugboat has moved in and has taken station along the port side of the *California*. Lieutenant M. J. Hannifan, USN, was the pilot who directed the movement of the ship from the floating dry dock. (A.D. Baker III collection) **Above left:** The *California* continues to back out of

floating dry dock, moving at a rate of all engines back one-third. Two diminutive landing craft, mechanized (LCMs) have come alongside port amidships to lend their power to the maneuvering of the ship out of dry dock. (A.D. Baker III collection) **Above right:** Six days after USS *California* departed from Espiritu, on 17 September 1944 the battleship (center foreground) is anchored in Seeadler Harbor, Manus Island, Papua New Guinea. It had joined the fleet preparing for the invasion of Leyte in the Philippines. (NARA)

The Battle of Surigao Strait

On 25 October 1944 *California* was one of the participants in history's final battleship versus battleship engagement. The allies put in motion a plan to invade Leyte in the central Philippines, the broader objective being to break the supply of fuel needed by the Japanese war machine. The Japanese strategy was to lure the Americans away by using the IJN carrier fleet as bait, and thus leave the landing force exposed, so that IJN surface forces under Vice Admirals Shoji Nishimura, Kiyohide Shima and Takeo Kurita could annihilate them. The Japanese 'Southern Force' consisting of the battleships *Yamashiro* and *Fuso*, the heavy cruiser *Mogami*, and four destroyers all under Nishimura were to strike through Surigao Strait.

There Nishimura's fleet ran afoul of the 7th Fleet Support Force, Task Groups 77.2 and 77.3, Rear Admiral Jesse Oldendorf commanding, flying his flag from the cruiser *Louisville*. Five of Oldenedorf's six venerable battleships, like *California*, were Pearl Harbor veterans. In addition to *California*, there were battleships *West Virginia*, *Maryland*, *Mississippi*, *Tennessee*, and *Pennsylvania*, plus four each heavy and light cruisers, 28 destroyers and 39 PT boats. The U.S. battleships had spent the past several days conducting shore bombardments, and the crews were well honed. Rear Admiral G.L. Weyler commanded the battle line from *Mississippi*. At about 3 am both Japanese battleships were struck by torpedoes fired by U.S. destroyers, with DD-680 *Melvin* sinking *Fuso*. At 0316 *West Virginia*'s radar picked up the remaining Japanese ships, and she opened fire at 0353 at a range of 22,800 yards, two minutes later *California* and *Tennessee* added their weight to the onslaught, *California* loosing 63 14-inch rounds at the enemy to starboard beginning at a range of 20,400 yards. At 0404 *California*, steaming at 15 knots, ceased fire and swung around, her main battery turrets pivoting to they could again be brought to bear on the enemy. At 0407 she resumed fire, two minutes later she checked fire, after firing a total of 63 14-inch rounds, and the Japanese southern force being routed. Nishimura's flagship *Yamashiro* sank about 0420, with him aboard. By dawn only two of Nishimura's ships remained, with *Mogami* being abandoned at 1047 and scuttled two hours later, leaving only *Shigure* as a survivor of the Japanese Southern force.

Above: One of the USS *California*'s Vought OS2U Kingfisher scout planes flies over Manus Island, Papua New Guinea, during the battleship's sojourn there in September 1944. In the upper left background are ships of the invasion fleet destined for Leyte. **Below right:** From Manus Island, USS *California* proceeded to Leyte Gulf in October 1944, taking up a firing position off Dulag, Leyte, in the predawn hours of 19 October. In this photo, three battleships are firing on shore targets, including *California* in the right background. (NARA, both) **Below:** In 1944 *California*'s Kingfisher aircraft were painted in the Navy's graded camouflage scheme of Semi Gloss Sea Blue (ANA 606), Intermediate Blue (ANA 608) and Insignia White (ANA 601).

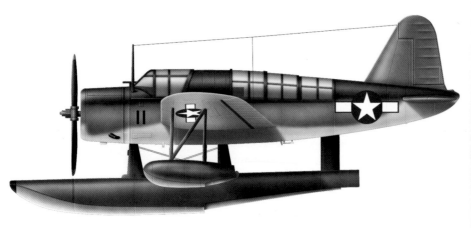

Top: In a photograph taken from USS *West Virginia* (BB-48) off Leyte on 19 October 1944, ships of Task Group 77.2 are arrayed for bombardment. In the center background, USS *Maryland* (BB-46) has just fired its main battery; *California* is to its right. **Above left:** A cameraman in one of USS *California*'s OS2U scout planes took this photo of the Dulag landing beach. Thanks in part to the fire support of the *California* and other ships, the landings on Leyte proceeded without major mishaps, and the troops advanced inland. **Above right:** Another photo taken from a Vought OS2U Kingfisher from USS *California* shows the Dulag landing sector. In the 20 October 1944 landings on Leyte, the main assault was on an 18-mile front spanning from Dulag to San Jose. (NARA, all)

Top left: The scout planes of the cruisers and battleships of the U.S. Fleet supplemented the reconnaissance work of carrier-based planes in World War II by taking photos such as this one of a Leyte landing zone taken from a *California* Vought OS2U. **Top right:** This aerial photograph taken from one of the USS *California*'s OS2U scout planes documents the front line of amtracks as it advanced through Area 6029 on Leyte. The line of mixed-model amphibious vehicles runs laterally across the center of the photo. **Above left:** USS *California* is receiving a replenishment of ammunition from a transport ship off Leyte. Adjacent to the twin 5-inch/38-caliber gun mount with guns elevated at the lower left is a sling full of ten 14-inch powder canisters. Antiaircraft crews are on watch. **Above Right:** In another photo taken during the same supply replenishment operation, crewmen on the forecastle deck of the *California* wrestle with a sling containing two 14-inch projectiles at the center of the photo, adjacent to the gun house of turret one, trained to starboard. (NARA, all)

Top left: USS *California* steams with Task Group 77.2 through Surigao Strait in the Philippines on 3 January 1945. A little over two months earlier, on 25 October 1944, the *California* had fought with distinction in these seas in the Battle of Surigao Strait. (A.D. Baker III collection) **Top right:** The *California* was providing fire support for the invasion of Lingayen Gulf on 6 January 1945 when, at 1720, a Japanese Mitsubishi A6M5 Model 52 made a suicide attack on the battleship, exploding against the mainmast tower, as seen at the center of this photograph. (NARA) **Above left:** In the aftermath of the suicide attack on USS *California* on 6 January 1945, antiaircraft gun crews watch the sky expectantly for further attacks. The A6M5 Zero struck the mainmast tower at the center of the photo, hitting it at the rear of the 05 level. (NARA) **Above right:** The damage to the mainmast tower is viewed from a closer perspective. The kamikaze strike knocked out the aft main-battery director at the top of the mainmast tower and the aft, or number-four, Mk. 37 secondary-battery director, to the right of the photo. (NARA)

Top left: In a photo of the *California's* mainmast tower from the front after the 6 January attack, above the port 36-inch searchlight on the tower is the number 3, indicating a large hole caused by a fragment through the 25-pound special treatment steel (STS). **Above left:** The kamikaze heavily damaged the aft Mk. 37 director, as seen from Sky Aft Control. As of 13 January, losses were listed as 45 killed, 155 wounded, and 3 missing in the attack, most of whom had been in the aft air-defense stations and exposed antiaircraft mounts. **Above right:** The breach the kamikaze plane made in the mainmast tower was located slightly to the port of the vertical centerline of the rear of the tower at the 05 level. The opening was approximately 6.5 feet square. The blast destroyed much of the interior of the tower. (NARA, all)

Top left: The effects of the blast caused by the kamikaze plane forward of the mainmast tower are viewed from the port searchlight platform looking down toward the main deck. Fragments and splinters hit structures up to 75 feet away from the site of the blast. **Top right:** The kamikaze strike on the mainmast tower caused the ship's bell to drop on the standard-compass platform; this damage is viewed from the 02 level. This platform was located on the 03 level between the smokestack and the mainmast tower. **Above left:** The twisted remains of a 20mm cannon from the Japanese Zero fighter plane that crashed into the *California* on 6 January 1945 is viewed on deck. The official USN report of the kamikaze attack established that the plane had only one such weapon installed. **Above right:** A piece of the frame of the kamikaze Zero that hit the mainmast tower lies on the deck of the *California*. To the upper left is a stack of lids for 40mm ammunition containers, while next to the fire hose to the upper center is a 40mm ammunition container. (NARA, all)

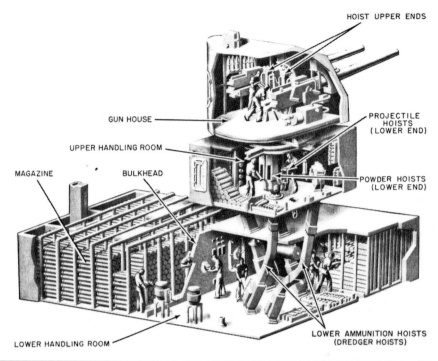

HOIST UPPER ENDS

GUN HOUSE

PROJECTILE HOISTS (LOWER END)

UPPER HANDLING ROOM

MAGAZINE   BULKHEAD

POWDER HOISTS (LOWER END)

LOWER HANDLING ROOM

LOWER AMMUNITION HOISTS (DREDGER HOISTS)

Top left: Some of the damage caused by the kamikaze strike is shown. Although the report of the attack established that the Zero carried an explosive charge, observers of the attack reported that they could see no bomb or explosive device underneath the plane.
Top right: Beneath each of the 5-inch/38-caliber gun mounts was a complete suite of handling rooms and magazines, connected to the mount via ammunition and powder hoists.

Above left: The damage in the interior of 5-inch/38-caliber gun mount number four is shown. The projectile that penetrated the front of the gun shield was determined to be a 5-inch antiaircraft common shell that a crew on another USN ship fired at the suicide plane.
Above right: This view from the outside of the 5-inch/38 gun mount number four shows the penetration through the mount's front armor by the 5-inch shell. (NARA, all)

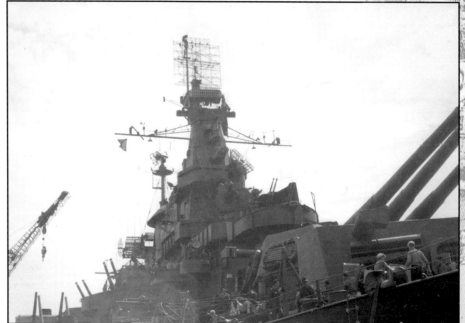

Above left: With her fire-control system seriously impaired and with one twin 5-inch gun mount out of commission from the kamikaze attack, it was necessary to sail the *California* to Navy Yard Puget Sound for repairs. This photo, taken at that yard on the day of the ship's arrival, 15 February 1945, shows the breach in the rear of the mainmast tower, upper right; the crumpled port searchlight platform; and a weld failure on the 04 level. **Above right:** Also taken on 15 February 1945 was this photo showing the front of

the aft Mk. 34 main-battery director and the Mk. 8 radar on top of it. Many of the 42 polyrods projecting from the front of the radar antenna have been bent, damaged, or completely broken off. **Top right:** The following series of views of USS *California* was taken on 20 April 1945, four days before the overhaul of the ship at the Navy Yard Puget Sound was completed. The SK "bedspring" air-search radar antenna was still present atop the foremast. (NARA, all)

Top left: The superstructure of the *California* is viewed from the starboard side. During the overhaul, the Mk. 4 radar antenna on each Mk. 37 secondary-battery director was replaced with a Mk. 12 antenna with a Mk. 22 parabolic antenna jutting from its right side. **Above left:** Another new radar feature introduced in the April 1945 refitting was an SP height-finding radar at the top of the mainmast. Below that antenna is the newly repaired mainmast tower and Mk. 34 main-battery director with a new FH radar antenna on top of it. **Above right:** The front of the *California*'s superstructure is viewed from above turret two at the Navy Yard Puget Sound on 20 April 1945. The forward Mk. 34 director retains the Mk. 8 radar antenna on top. To each side of the superstructure, the new radar antennas on top of the Mk. 37 directors are visible from several angles, with the Mk 22 parabolic antenna prominent above the starboard director. (NARA, all)

Above left: Several antennas installed during the early-1945 refitting are present in this view of the superstructure from the starboard side. Jutting from the front of Main-Battery Fire Control, one level below the Mk. 34 director, is a TDY antenna, below which is a Mk. 27 radar antenna. Jutting from the front of the support structure for that antenna is a masthead light. **Above right:** In a view of the upper reaches of the foremast from the starboard side, at the top is the SG surface-search radar antenna. Below and to the port side of the SG antenna is an identification friend or foe (IFF) "ski-pole" antenna. Also below the SG is the SK air-search radar antenna, nicknamed the "bedspring antenna." To the lower right is the Mk. 34 main-battery director. (NARA, both)

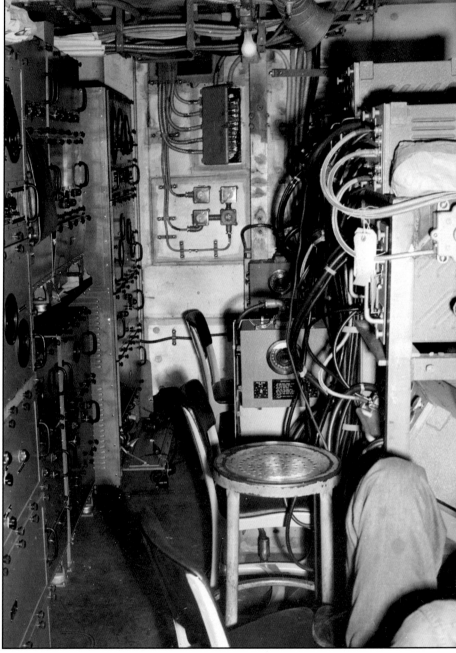

Left: In another photo taken at Navy Yard Puget Sound on 20 April 1945, the SP height-finding radar antenna and the associated service platform at the top of the mainmast are viewed from the starboard beam. Ladder rungs run up the side of the mainmast. To the right is the smokestack, and to the left are the newly repaired mainmast tower and aft Mk.

34 director. (NARA) **Right:** As on any U.S. battleship, there were numerous radar rooms on the USS *California*. Shown here is starboard radar room number 12, in a photograph taken at Navy Yard Puget Sound on 23 April 1945. To the lower right, a member of the crew is lying back to get out of the way of the photographer. (NARA)

Above left: The early-1945 refitting at Navy Yard Puget Sound included a number of new radar installations, some of which already have been discussed. Seen here is a newly installed Mk. 27 radar antenna on the gun house of turret number three. It is on the right side below the splinter shield atop the turret. **Top right:** The SP height-finding radar is viewed from the rear, with the foremast and forward Mk. 34 director in the background.

The SP radar provided accurate data on the altitude of aerial targets, to allow more accurate antiaircraft fire against enemy aircraft. **Above right:** This is the switchboard in *California*'s secondary-battery plot. If the directors above decks were the eyes of the fire-control system, secondary-battery plot was the nerve center of secondary battery, containing computers, stable elements, and communications gear. (NARA, all)

California steams in Puget Sound on 25 April 1945, one day after her overhaul was completed. She now had Measure 21 camouflage, consisting of Navy Blue (5-N) on vertical surfaces above the boot topping and Deck Blue (20-B) on horizontal surfaces. (A.D. Baker III collection)

Top: *California* is viewed from the starboard beam on 25 April 1945. The national ensign on the gaff is at half-mast as a mark of mourning and respect for President Franklin Delano Roosevelt, who had died less than two weeks earlier, on 12 April. **Above left:** The USS *California* is viewed from over the bow in Puget Sound, Washington, on 25 April 1945. The ship got underway at 0838 that morning on a post-repair trial run. Aboard was an observation party from Navy Yard Puget Sound. **Above right:** The ship is observed from dead astern as she makes 20 knots in Puget Sound on 25 April 1945. No aircraft were aboard, but in three days the ship would receive a complement of new scout planes to replace the OS2U Kingfishers: Curtiss SC Sea Hawks. (A.D. Baker III collection, all)

California cruises in Puget Sound on 25 April 1945. The mainmast tower and the surrounding exposed gun mounts, the scene of so much death and destruction in the 6 January 1945 kamikaze attack, were now fully repaired and functional. (A.D. Baker III collection)

The following series of photographs of USS *California* at anchor in Sinclair Inlet off the Navy Yard Puget Sound on 28 April 1945 was taken on the day before the ship departed from that facility. The dark area on the bow is from the shadow cast by the hull overhang. (A.D. Baker III collection)

USS California (BB44) 1945

Following her early 1945 overhaul, *California* returned to the fleet wearing Camouflage Measure 21, 5-N Navy Blue on vertical surfaces above the boot topping, and 20-B Deck Blue on horizontal surfaces.

The *California*'s battleship number, 44, now was painted in White over the Navy Blue on both sides of the bow and the stern. Onboard now were two of the ship's new observation planes, Curtiss SC-1 Seahawks, painted in three-color camouflage schemes. (A.D. Baker III collection)

Top left: The early-1945 modernization of the *California* brought with it numerous upgrades to the fire-control systems. For example, although not easily discernible in these photos, there now were radar directors for the 40mm antiaircraft battery at various locations. (NARA) **Top right:** The 20mm gun batteries had been changed during the 1945 refitting. For example, the two galleries of 20mm guns on the forecastle deck abeam of turret two, along with their splinter shields, had been removed. Three twin 20mm guns were now forward of turret one. (NARA) **Above:** A close comparison of this photo of the starboard side of *California* with photos of the ship before the early-1945 repairs and renovations reveals some changes were made to the structures between the mainmast tower and the aft Mk. 37 secondary-battery director. (A.D. Baker III collection)

Top left: On the quarterdeck above the motor launch moored to the *California's* side was a newly redesigned splinter shield for the 20mm guns. In addition, the previous, single 20mm gun mounts in this area had been replaced by twin 20mm antiaircraft gun mounts. **Top right:** The *California* is viewed from astern on 28 April 1945. A close inspection of the image reveals the number 26 on the fuselage of the Seahawk to the left. The other plane bore number 25. In the left background is the hammerhead crane of Navy Yard Puget Sound. (A.D. Baker III collection, both) **Right:** Like the Kingfishers before them, *California's* Curtiss Seahawk aircraft were painted in the Navy's graded camouflage scheme of Semi Gloss Sea Blue (ANA 606), Intermediate Blue (ANA 608) and Insignia White (ANA 601)

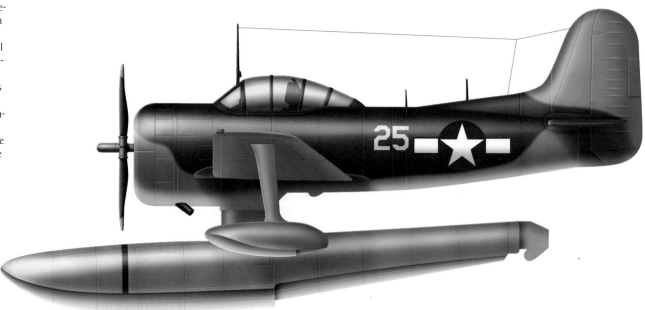

Top left: While proceeding to Pearl Harbor on 13 May 1945, one of USS *California's* Curtiss SC-1 Seahawk scout planes, number 25, is launched from the catapult. Powering the aircraft was a Wright R-1820-62 turbosupercharged engine rated at 1,350 horsepower. **Top right:** The *California's* other Curtiss SC-1, number 26, also took a turn at a launching at sea on 13 May 1945. Here, the plane is proceeding at wavetop level, flaps lowered. Unlike the Vought OS2U with its two-man crew, the SC-1 made do with only the pilot. **Above left:** As SC-1 number 25 rests on a dolly on the fantail of *California*

as SC-1 number 26 taxis in for recovery. The ship has made a turn across the wind, creating a smooth patch of sea called a slick on which the plane could make what was called a Charlie landing. Note the AN/APS-4 radar pod under the starboard wing of aircraft 25. **Above right:** One of *California's* SC-1s has touched down on the sea and is taxiing up to a sled being towed by the ship. A hook on the bottom of the center float of the plane will engage the sled, after which the sled and plane will be brought alongside the ship for recovery. (NARA, all)

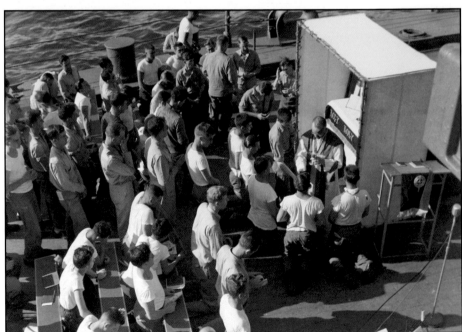

Top left: In May 1945 the crewmen of a quad 40mm antiaircraft gun mount on the *California* relax at their stations. Canvas covers are secured over the receivers and the automatic ammunition feeds of the guns to keep corrosive saltwater out of the inner works.

Top right: Sports were important for morale on Navy ships, and boxing always was a favorite. Here, during a fight night on the USS *California* while anchored at Ulithi Atoll on 11 June 1945, two boxers have taken the fight outside of the ring, to the delight of spectators.

Above left: Sunday religious services were a traditional part of life on a Navy ship. Here, crewmen of the *California* attend a service on deck on a sunny 10 June 1945. The chaplain is at a lectern to the side of a portable altar. In poor weather, services were held inside.

Above right: Sailors receive communion at the same 10 June 1945 worship service. The photograph was taken from the roof of a main-battery turret's gun house. To the far right is the forward facet of the housing for the right objective of the rangefinder. (NARA, all)

Top left: The destroyer USS *Cowell* (DD-547) approaches USS *California* off her starboard stern during the summer of 1945. The diminutive destroyers played a crucial role in any fleet or convoy, providing antisubmarine, antiaircraft, and anti-ship protection. **Top right:** Signalmen of the USS *California* go about their tasks on the signal bridge. The man viewing through the telescope to the right is likely receiving a blinkered Morse code signal from another ship. To the rear is a quad 40mm gun mount, ammunition loaded. **Above left:** With their large fuel capacity, battleships frequently provided fuel for smaller ships at sea. While cruising with Task Group 32.15 southeast of Okinawa on the afternoon of 25 June 1945, USS *California* refuels the destroyer escort USS *Paul G. Baker* (DE-642). **Above right:** According to the original caption of this series of photos, the *Paul G. Baker* rammed the *California* during the refueling operation. Although the *Baker* appears to be having a rough time of it, the *California's* war diary mentions no serious collision. (NARA, all)

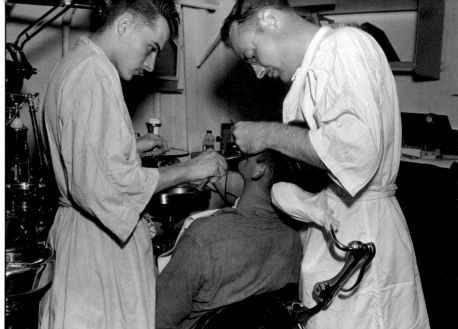

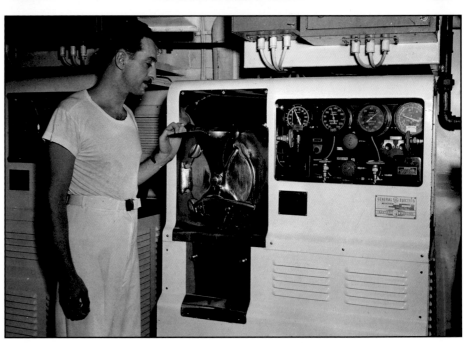

Top left: Crewmen of the USS *California* enjoy a meal on 4 July 1945. Boatswain's Mate 2nd Class (BM2) John Field, second from left, hams it up with a turkey leg as Musician 3rd Class Joseph F. Gregorio, BM2 Thomas A. Bradley, and BM1 Plulyo Slade look on. (NARA)
Top right: Like other USN capital ships, USS *California* had state-of-the-art medical facilities, including a fully staffed and well-equipped dental office. In this 3 July 1943 photo, a ship's dentist and his assistant perform a routine procedure on a sailor. (NARA) **Above**

left: Some of the most popular spots in the *California* were the snack bars, where sailors could purchase "gedunk," slang for ice cream, sodas, potato chips, and other junk food. Here, men behind the counter are dispensing fountain drinks to a line of thirsty sailors. (NARA) **Above right:** One of the luxuries a U.S. Navy battleship of World War II could offer its crew was freshly made ice cream. This piece of machinery on USS *California* was a General Electric/Bastian-Blessing ice cream freezer. It had a five-gallon capacity. (NARA)

Top left: A photographer aboard USS *California* took this photo of her sister ship, USS *Tennessee*, in Buckner Bay (Nakagusuku Bay), Okinawa, on 17 July 1945. The following day, these ships would evacuate the bay with Task Force 32 in order to dodge an imminent typhoon. **Top right:** While covering mine-clearing operations of Task Force 32 in the East China Sea west of Okinawa on 25 July 1945, members of Sky Control scan for enemy aircraft. In the foreground is a Mk. 51 director, equipped with a Mk. 14 computing gun sight. **Above left:** Crews of several 40mm gun mounts fire at towed target sleeves during an antiaircraft exercise on the *California* on 29 July 1945. During the exercise, the 40mm guns expended a total of 2,069 rounds. To the lower left is a Mk. 51 director. **Above right:** Crews of the *California*'s 5-inch/38-caliber gun mounts conduct drills on loading machines on the ship. These were non-firing apparatuses that had a breech, rammer assembly, loading tray, and fuse setters that functioned like the actual ones. (NARA, all)

Top left: The long wartime road of USS *California* from her sinking at Pearl Harbor through her resurrection and operational service came to its close on V-J Day, 15 August 1945 (14 August in the United States). Crewmembers celebrate the victory on V-J Day. **Top right:** In another photo taken on the *California* on V-J Day, sailors enjoy the satisfaction of victory over Japan and the knowledge that they have survived the worst the Empire could give them. At this time, the ship was anchored in San Pedro Bay, the Philippines. **Above left:** Victory celebrations continue aboard USS *California* at San Pedro Bay. Underneath the boat chocks in the foreground, a band is playing. In the background, the center and port floats of one of the Curtiss SC-1 Seahawk scout planes are in view. **Above right:** The band pauses between songs on the fantail of the USS *California* during the victory celebration in San Pedro Bay. The catapult is partially hidden in the background, and to the right are the lower part of the aircraft crane and the national ensign on the flagstaff. (NARA, all)

Top left: Two crewmen on the USS *California* are preparing to shoot a line over to the ship in the background, so that a larger line can be attached and hauled across. The *California* had returned to Buckner Bay, Okinawa, by the time this photo was taken on 8 September 1945. **Top right:** Adjacent to a quad 40mm gun tub and boat chocks on the *California*, preparations are being made to send a diver (center) overboard. Above the diver is a sling connected to a hoist, which will be used to lift him over the side and lower him into the water. **Above left:** Members of the crew of USS *California* are lined up on the foredeck during an inspection by Vice Admiral Jesse B. Oldendorf at Wakanoura-wan (now Wakaura Bay), Japan, on 24 September 1945. On either side of the deck are paravanes and their derricks. **Above right:** USS *California* rides at anchor off Wakayama, Japan, 29 September 1945. The battleship, along with her sister ship the *Tennessee*, was there to provide cover for the landing of the occupation forces of the Sixth Army at Wakanoura-wan. (NARA, all)

USS *California* is viewed from her port side at Wakayama, Japan. While the *California* was anchored, the crew kept busy by conducting training drills and performing general upkeep on the ship and its systems. Within a few days, the ship would proceed to Yokosuka before departing from Japan with Task Group 50.5 for the United States by way of the Cape of Good Hope. (NARA)

Top left: *California* took a westerly course to the United States because she had been reassigned to the Atlantic Coast and the hull blisters added during the war made her too wide to navigate the Panama Canal. Here, the ship stops at Colombo, Ceylon, in late October 1945. **Top right:** A Royal Navy officer boards the USS *California* during her sojourn in Colombo, Ceylon (now Sri Lanka), in October 1945. This was an informal visit because both the visiting Americans and their British hosts waived all official visits during the ship's stay in port. **Above left:** Visiting dignitaries come aboard USS *California* at Colombo, Ceylon. In the immediate background is a gallery of twin 20mm gun mounts, their barrels raised and with covers installed. Farther back is a quad 40mm gun mount, with its director tub to the left. **Above right:** On 2 November 1945 a reception was held for visitors aboard the *California* while anchored at Colombo, Ceylon. It was held under a cover with the 14-inch guns of turret four overhead. To the left is the catapult, being used to hold a loudspeaker and drinks. (NARA, all)

After departing from Colombo, in early November 1945 the *California* crossed the Indian Ocean en route to Capetown, South Africa. Here, the ship is navigating a rough stretch of ocean, waves breaking over the bow. Antiaircraft guns are tightly covered. (NARA)

Top left: A group of South African naval and army personnel was aboard USS *California* for the voyage from Colombo, Ceylon, to Capetown. Some of them are on the fantail in this photograph, apparently observing an aircraft fly-past or exhibition in the open ocean. **Top right:** The Jolly Roger has been struck from the mainmast of the *California* in early November 1945, and that can mean only one thing: the ship is crossing the equator, and that ancient maritime tradition, a crossing-the-line, or Neptune party, is underway. **Above left:** The Neptune party was a rite of initiation for Pollywogs: members of the crew who were crossing the equator for the first time. It was accompanied by much pomp and costuming, with King Neptune and Davy Jones and other luminaries presiding over the ceremonies. **Above right:** Musicians strike up a tune during the Neptune party on USS *California*. Pollywogs were expected to sing and recite poetry for Davy Jones once he made his appearance. Trusty Shellbacks, sailors who previously had crossed the equator, enjoy the show. (NARA, all)

Top left: On the fantail, several Pollywogs sing a song accompanied by guitar. Outrageous garb was the order of the day for Pollywogs and the members of King Neptune's Court. In the background is one of the USS *California*'s Curtiss SC-1 Seahawk scout planes. **Above left:** The leering character with eye patch and skulls and crossbones was likely Davy Jones, who, with his retinue, was whipping the Pollywogs of USS *California*

into shape. The loinclothed Pollywogs to the left have been daubed with some sacramental substance. **Above right:** Officers and t-shirted crewmen who already have crossed the equator and been initiated as Trusty Shellbacks line the gun tubs, turret roofs, and forecastle deck to observe the initiation of Pollywogs during USS *California*'s Neptune party on 3 November 1945. (NARA, all)

Top left: Participants in the *California*'s Neptune party during the voyage from Ceylon to South Africa pose on the fantail next to the catapult and a Curtiss SC-1 Seahawk. Pollywogs who passed the initiation were issued certificates that they were now Trusty Shellbacks. **Top right:** USS *California* approaches the harbor at Capetown, South Africa, on an official visit on 15 November 1945. The photograph was taken from the starboard side of the fantail, with one of its Curtiss Seahawk scout planes, number 23, in the view.**Above**

left: Sailors take a break on the starboard side of the forecastle of USS *California* around the time of the ship's return to the United States after the end of World War II. Jutting from the side of turret number one is its right rangefinder housing. (NARA) **Above right:** Civilian guests are welcomed onboard USS *California* during her visit to Capetown in November 1945. While in port, the ship hosted several dinner parties and dances for local dignitaries as well as open houses for the local citizenry on two afternoons. (NARA, all)

On 18 November 1945, USS *California* is moored to a dock in Duncan Basin, Capetown, Union of South Africa. During the battleship's four-day visit to this port, the local citizenry reportedly demonstrated much hospitality to the officers and crew. (NARA)

Top left: While at Capetown, the ships' sports teams of Task Group 50.5 engaged in friendly athletic competitions with South African teams. Seen here at Capetown is USS *California*'s boxing team, posing with their trophies by the catapult on the fantail. (NARA)
Top right: Another view of the forecastle of USS *California* was taken from above the forward quad 40mm antiaircraft mount on the superstructure. Bedding is hanging over the rails of the forecastle to dry, and crewmen are scrubbing what appear to be hose sections. (NARA) **Above left:** An armorer is loading 20mm ammunition into magazines in a compartment on the 04 level of the mainmast tower of USS *California*. The refillable drum-shaped magazines will be distributed to ready-service ammunition lockers near the 20mm antiaircraft gun mounts. (NARA) **Above right:** Although homeward bound, *California* was still a warship, and as such drills and maintenance continued. Two members of the *California*'s secondary battery swab a 5-inch/38-caliber gun with a rammer. Cleaning the guns was a necessary chore to keep the bores from fouling from powder residue and to prevent them from corroding in the saltwater environment. (NARA)

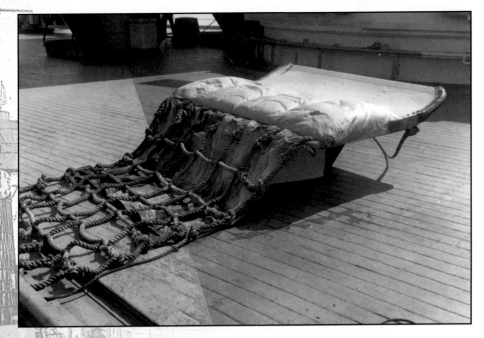

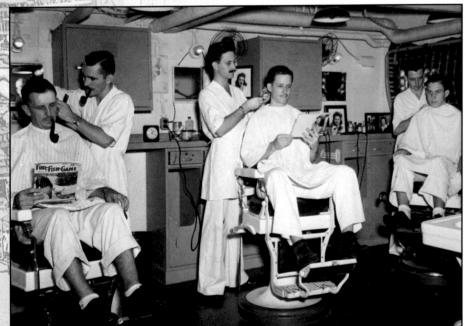

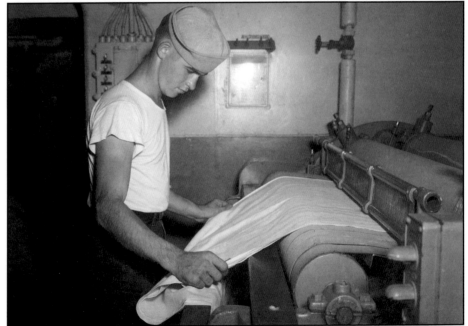

Top left: A sled used in recovering USS *California*'s scout planes is lying on deck. The ship towed the sled through water, and a hook on the taxiing plane's center float would catch the woven-rope net attached to the sled. Two skegs on the sled provided stability. (NARA) **Top right:** The sled is positioned right-side-up, with the front of the sled to the left. On top of the sled was cushioning. The net for catching the scout plane's center float trailed to the rear of the sled. Under the sled are metal boxes for supporting it in this position. (NARA)

Above left: The barbershop of the USS *California* was a busy spot, with hundreds of officers and sailors frequently requiring haircuts and trims. The sitter to the left reads a copy of Fur-Fish-Game magazine. Decorating the shop are photos of wives and girlfriends. (NARA) **Above right:** A laundryman named Remaski on USS *California* guides a piece of fabric through a mechanical press in 1945. This equipment facilitated ironing large quantities of clothing and fabric goods without the time-consuming process of hand-ironing. (NARA)

California General Data - 1919

Builder: Mare Island Naval Shipyard
Laid Down: 25 October 1916
Launched: 29 November 1919
Commissioned: 10 August 1921
Nickname: "The Prune Barge"
Dimensions: 624 feet, 5 inches length overall
Waterline Length: 600 feet
Maximum Beam: 97 feet, 6 inches
Maximum Draft: 31 feet
Displacement: 32,300 long tons standard
Cost: $65,844,966

Armor Protection

Total Armor Weight: 14,541.8 tons
Belt: 6 inches to 13.5 inches
Bulkheads: 13.5 inches
Decks: 70lb. Special Treatment Steel (STS) + 70lb Nickel Steel
Aft over steering; 180lb STS + 70lb Nickel Steel
Turret: Faceplates, 18 inches; roof, 5 inches; side, 10 inches; rear, 9 inches
Barbettes: 13 inches
Conning Tower: 16 inches sides; 6 inches on top

Machinery

Total Weight: 1,862.3 tons
Boilers: Eight Bureau Express
Turbines: Two General Electric
Shaft Horsepower: 28,500 maximum ahead
Maximum Speed: 21.0 knots
Fuel Capacity, Design; 4,656 tons of Bunker C Fuel Oil, emergency
Endurance: 10 knots: 20,500 nautical miles
Propellers: Four
Rudders: one, balanced

Complement

1,083 total (57 officers; 1,026 enlisted)

Armament

Main Battery: 12 14-inch, 50-caliber Mark IV-1
Secondary Battery: 14 5-inch, 51-caliber, Mark VIII
Antiaircraft Battery: 4 3-inch, 50-caliber Mark X-2
Torpedo tubes: 2 21-inch, Mark III-3
Landing gun: 1 3-inch, 23-caliber Mark XI
Machine Guns: 25 Browning .30-caliber Model 1918; 12 Lewis .30-caliber, Model 1917
Rifles: 350 Springfield, .30-caliber Model 1930
Pistols: 123 Colt, .45-caliber, Model 1911

California General Data - 1942 Rebuild

Builder: Puget Sound Naval Shipyard
Rebuild completed: 16 January 1944
Decommissioned: 14 February 1947
Struck: 1 March 1959
Honors and awards: Seven Battle Stars
Fate: Sold for scrap, 10 July 1959
Dimensions: 624 feet 5 inches length overall
Waterline Length: 600 feet
Maximum Beam: 114 feet
Maximum Draft: 33 feet 1 inch
Full Load Displacement: 40,354 long tons

Armor Protection

Cruiser conning tower with 5-inch thick armor installed, second deck armor increased from 5 to 7 inches. The five-inch thick turret roof armor was replaced with new plates 7 inches thick, as well.

Machinery

Total Weight: 1,862.3 tons
Boilers: Eight Bureau Express
Turbines: Two General Electric
Shaft Horsepower: 32,500 maximum ahead
Maximum Speed: 20.6 knots
Fuel Capacity, full load: 4,700 tons of Bunker C Fuel Oil
Propellers: Four
Rudders: one, balanced

Complement

2,243 total (114 officers; 2,129 enlisted)

Armament

Main Battery: 12 14-inch, 50-caliber Mark IV-1
Secondary Battery: 16 5-inch, 38-caliber
Antiaircraft Battery: 10 quad 40mm; 43 20mm

Philadelphia, drydock and reserve

While *California* was not present in Tokyo Bay for the Japanese surrender ceremonies on 2 September, one month and one day later she, along with *Tennessee*, steamed into the bay, mooring at Buoy 4 of the Yokosuka Naval Base. Liberty parties went ashore—actually the second time sightseers from *California* had been on Japanese soil, the previous expedition being at Wakayama/Wakanoura on 22 September. As welcome as it was to be ashore, Tokyo was not where the crew truly wanted to be—which was home.

Orders back to the United States did come, but incredibly, both *California* and her sister ship *Tennessee* were ordered to Philadelphia, despite having spent the last two decades on the west coast. The post-Pearl Harbor refit of both ships had rendered them too broad to transit the Panama Canal, meaning that to reach Philadelphia the ships would have to sail either around the tip of South America, or via the Indian Ocean and Africa.

The decision was made to sail through the Indian Ocean, and on 15 October 1945, *California* and the rest of Task Group 50.5 began the 16,000-mile trip to Philadelphia. Originally, Vice Admiral Jesse Oldendorf and his staff were to sail with the Task Group, but were instead directed to remain in Japan. Oldendorf sent this message to the *California*:

> "Officers and men of the U.S.S. California; We have been shipmates and have traveled a long, rough road together. Our efforts have been crowned with success. Now we have reached a parting of the ways. May your return voyage and homecoming give you all the happiness you so richly deserve. Au Revoir."

The long voyage was interrupted by sightseeing ports of call, including Singapore and Cape Town, finally reaching the entrance to Delaware Bay off Cape May at noon 6 December 1945. The next day, four years after she was attacked at Pearl Harbor, *California* tied up at Pier 2, Philadelphia Naval Shipyard.

On 8 May 1946 *California* was backed into Drydock 1 at a slight angle. Next, *Tennessee* was pushed in, bow first, at an overlapping angle. The drydock was pumped out, and the sister ships came to rest on keel blocks, where they would remain for years. *California* was placed out of commission on 14 February 1947. Her weapons and machinery were carefully preserved, and her spaces sealed. Dehumidification equipment drew moisture from the air, retarding deterioration of the interior spaces.

California, her sister *Tennessee*, and the other Pearl Harbor survivors that were deemed too new to be used in the atom bomb tests at Bikini awaited a call to arms that never came. The Korean War brought about the return to action of only the new *Iowa* class battleships, the venerable *California* and her pre-WWII sisters remaining in a deep sleep. *California* was to remain laid up in reserve until 1 March 1959, when finally she was deemed obsolete, and was struck from the Naval Register.

With the handwriting on the wall as far back as 1956, there was brief consideration of returning the warship to her namesake state for preservation as a war memorial, as the Lone Star State had done with the *Texas*. Alas, *California*'s girth, which had caused the 16,000 mile voyage home, again came into play. Because of the inability to transit the Panama Canal, the voyage from Philadelphia to *California* would be a 15,000-mile journey. Her machinery long idled, no consideration was given to steaming back to her home state, and a tow of that distance was estimated to cost over $3 million. Accordingly preservation plans were scrapped, and so too soon would be the *California*.

On 10 July *California* was sold for scrap to the Bethlehem Steel Company for $859,999, and on 14 July left Philadelphia under tow, arriving at the breaker's yard in Baltimore on 16 July.

Top right: USS *California*'s final destination in the return voyage from Japan was Philadelphia, where the ship arrived, quite significantly, on 7 December: four years to the day after her ordeal at Pearl Harbor. This photo is thought to show the ship approaching Philadelphia. **Above right:** Following her arrival at Philadelphia, the *California* spent the following winter docked at the Navy Yard, her crew preparing her for long-term storage. During that period, a destroyer escort rammed the *California* at her stern, as shown in this photo. (NARA, both)

In this undated photo of the *California* docked at Philadelphia Navy Yard, measures to place the ship in "mothballs" are apparent. The 14-inch guns and some of the 40mm mounts were encased in watertight sealing materials. The 20mm guns had been removed. (NARA)

Above left: The USS *California* enjoyed many distinctions: flagship of the Battle Fleet/Pacific Fleet for two decades; sunk at Pearl Harbor only to be resurrected and sent to battle the Japanese; the last battleship to be built on the West Coast; and many more. However, after World War II, the ship was placed in long-term storage (or "mothballs"), as seen here, and was scrapped in 1959. (NARA)

Above right: Displayed on the Capitol grounds in Sacramento is *California*'s bell, removed in 1949 while the ship was in reserve, and presented to the state governor on 27 October by the Mare Island Naval Shipyard commandant, Rear Admiral H.E. Haven.